The Thirty-Six stratagems

——China Ancient Wisdom Training Program

A kind of bedside book for training the Wisdom.

An effective guide to knowing just the right people.

Modern enterprise management collection.

CONTENTS

Introduction

16.Letting the enemy off in order to catch him

17.Bait a piece of jade with a brick

18.Capturing the ringleader first in order to capture all the followers

19.Take away the firewood under the cooking pot

20.Muddling the water to catch the fish; fishing in troubled waters

21.getting away like the cicada sloughing its skin

22.Catching the thief by closing / blocking his escape route

23.Befriending the distant enemy while attacking a nearby enemy

24.Obtain safe passage to conquer the enemy

25.Stealing the beams and pillars and replacing them with rotten timbers

26.Reviling / abusing the locust tree while pointing to the mulberry

27.Feigning madness without becoming insane

28.Pull down the ladder after ascent

29.Deck the tree with bogus blossom

30.turning from the guest into the host or Host and guest reversed

Bibliography

About the author

Thanks

Introduction

"The Thirty-Six stratagems" is a book about ancient Chinese military tactics and strategies. This stratagem is an important part of ancient Chinese military history. It represents the wisdom of military strategists.

Some people think that "The Thirty-Six stratagems" were not written by just one person. The book probably came from popular Chinese stories, history, and expressions.

Certainly, the exact date and authorship of "The Thirty-Six stratagems" cannot be determined. It is believed to have been compiled during the late Ming Dynasty to the early Qing Dynasty.

The original text of "The Secret of War - Thirty-Six Strategies" is quite short. It only has 138 Chinese characters. It merely names each stratagem followed by a brief explanation.

Still, understanding and using these 138 words might need more explanations and changes. It is a task that relies heavily on human wisdom to practice.

"The Thirty-Six stratagems" were once about many strategies, not just exactly 36. However, the term "Thirty-Six Strategies" already existed. People collected and compiled different strategies from ancient Chinese folklore. They summarized these strategies into 36 to match the book's content and title. There are many other tactics not included in this book, like "killing two birds with one stone." Other examples include "making things worse" and "scaring others with extreme actions." Some examples involve "pretending ignorance to catch a clever person."

Every ethnic group has its own thinking template.

Long ago, people shared their wisdom through stories, sayings, poems, and codes. Jews see the Talmud as a wise source. It contains ideas and regulations, which are their nation's survival rules. They summarized them during their long exile.

Campfire stories are a great way to share wisdom and thinking templates worldwide. The stories "The Farmer and the Snake","One Thousand and One Nights"and "Stone Soup" have important lessons for people to learn.

Chinese wisdom is widely recognized in the world. Let's start with the "Thirty-Six Strategies" today:

Chinese culture has a long history of over five thousand years. The Chinese people have contributed the Great Wall and traditional Chinese medicine to the world. They have also invented many things, like Qigong and calligraphy. Within the vast literature, there are writings about "wisdom" and "stratagem" that stand out.

The book "The Analects of Confucius" contains the wisdom of ancient sage Confucius on governing.

The ancient book "Zhouyi" is about the great wisdom of calculation, including politics, economy, the world and life ... Its connotation is profound and profound.

In addition, there are other works that can enlighten people with wisdom, like "The Tao Te Ching" and "The Book of Songs".

Chinese people are skilled at using smart strategies to outwit opponents instead of relying on strength. They have a knack for subduing others through strategic thinking. Therefore, China's ancient sages left so many books about "Strategies".

China has always been a wise man. China people's wisdom comes from their diligence and diligence ... China people also attach great importance to wisdom. Everyone hopes that their children can become "future Zhuge Liang", "intelligent stars" and "divine operators" who can give prediction results in advance ...

The book "The Thirty-Six stratagems"helps Western readers understand human nature under extreme stress.

After the First World War, the defeated Emperor William saw this wonderful book in prison, and when he finished reading it, he was amazed. Then he sighed loudly: "If I had read this book earlier, I wouldn't have ended up in such a fiasco!" "

At West Point, the military academy, there is a course on studying "Sun Tzu's Art of War". In American prisons, the book "The Thirty-Six stratagems" is banned, and prisoners cannot learn from it.

The times encourage wisdom in love, enlightenment, development, and creation as life's goal. People's wisdom is not innate and needs to be learned and used for reference. Learn from present and ancient people; Learn from life and practice; Learn from the crystallization of wisdom left by sages and masters ... As a reader of this book, will you take the time to learn the wisdom of ancient saints in China?

In the past, people didn't understand playing tricks and thought it was insincere to treat others that way. I think people with bad intentions do this. It seems like a tactic for war, not for regular life. This is really a mistake and understanding. You can use strategies in politics, economy, diplomacy, and life. To be wise, learn wisdom to improve your character.

Next, this book will analyze and explain 36 kinds of strategies. I hope you can slowly understand the deep meaning and use it well. Learn the positive and good side in the book. I hope it helps your work and study.

text

1、 Cross the sea under camouflage

It means to use camouflage, take advantage of a rare opportunity, and take a surprise action when the other party is not paying attention, so that the other party is caught off guard.

According to legend, the Emperor of the Tang Dynasty in China led 300,000 troops and left the capital Chang 'an for an expedition to the eastern part of Liao. When the army arrived at the seaside, the emperor of the Tang Dynasty looked up and saw the boundless sea, which seemed to be a shipwreck and made him anxious. When the general named Xue Rengui saw this situation, he had a stratagem: he invited the emperor to enter a colorful camp that had already been prepared by the seaside, assuming that he would figure it out by himself. Then ordered the civil and military officials to go into the tent to drink and have fun. At that time, music accompanied everywhere, and the wine was fragrant. This situation actually made the emperor forget his sorrow and immerse himself in joy. Later, when everyone was drinking and having fun, the emperor suddenly heard a choppy sound outside the tent, so he quickly opened the tent and looked out. Only then did I find myself crossing the sea with 300,000 troops, and I was about to reach the coast. It turned out that Xue Rengui was worried that the emperor would give up marching eastward because of the sea barrier, so he commanded an army to cross the sea without telling him. Because the emperor is also called "the son of heaven" in China, it is called "deceiving the son of heaven to cross the sea".

Cross the sea under camouflage is to use camouflage as a cover; A stratagem of taking advantage of opportunities and taking advantage of people unprepared to achieve success. That is, pretending to take action on the outside to keep the other side alert, but actually taking no action. Such repeated disguises make the other party mistakenly think that this is just a bluff, and slowly slack off and relax their vigilance. At this time, immediately seize the negligence of the other party, take advantage of it and give the enemy a fatal blow. The key to this stratagem lies in the word "hide". If you hide it from the past, you will be successful. If you don't hide it from the past, it will be self-defeating. However, "cheating" is not the ultimate goal, but a necessary means of "crossing the sea".

There are many cases of camouflage, which can be divided into the following categories:

First, the stealth. That is, hide your tracks. If we hide our whereabouts, then the other party can't judge the direction and position of our actions. In this case, when the other party is in the light and we are in the dark, we can move freely and flexibly. For example, heads of state sometimes use body double to protect themselves in order to prevent assassination and beheading by other countries, which is also a kind of "crossing the sea".

Second, transfer audio and video. That is, turn the other party's attention to the public action, and make it ignore the hidden private action in this public action. If one action is used to cover up another action, then the other party will be confused, which will lead to certain cognitive misunderstandings. It is convenient for me to act in the blind area of the other party without being discovered.

Do you know the legend that Troy, the ancient Greek city-state, was attacked by Greek troops?

The Greek army that attacked Troy failed after years of siege, so they came up with a plan to enter the city.

The Greek army built a huge wooden horse and hid its soldiers in it. Trojan horse is lifelike in appearance, just like a gift or sacrifice. Then, the Greek army pretended to retreat, leaving this huge wooden horse as their "surrender gift".

After seeing the Trojan horse, the Trojans mistakenly thought that the Greeks had left and they had won, so they brought the Trojan horse into the city-state and celebrated their victory. However, in the dead of night, Greek soldiers climbed out of the hidden Trojan horse and opened the gate to let other Greek soldiers enter Troy.

The Trojans were attacked by the Greek army unsuspecting, which led to the fall of Troy. This story tells us, don't trust the enemy's surface easily, but always be alert to hidden threats and remain vigilant.

2. Relieve the state of Zhao by besieging the state of Wei

When the enemy is too strong to be attacked directly, then attack something he holds dear. Know that he cannot be superior in all things. Somewhere there is a gap in the armour, a weakness that can be attacked instead.

The idea here is to avoid a head-on battle with a strong enemy, and instead strike at his weakness elsewhere. This will force the strong enemy to retreat in order to support his weakness. Battling against the now tired and low-morale enemy will give a much higher chance of success.

The art of war says: use the enemy's elite to attack other countries, and when the two sides are deadlocked, take the opportunity to capture the enemy's homeland; When the enemy rushed back to the country to save themselves, it was the practice of Sun Bin, a great strategist in ancient China, to ambush them head-on and destroy them.

The story of saving Zhao from Wei is as follows: Wei and Zhao were two countries in the Central Plains of ancient China during the Warring States Period. Wei's army besieged Handan city, the capital of Zhao. Zhao asked Qi for help, and the King of Qi appointed Tian Ji as the general, and Sun Bin as the military staff, sending troops to save Zhao. Tian Ji wanted to lead troops directly to save Handan city of Zhao, while Sun Bin advocated to lead troops to besiege the capital girder of Wei, and Wei's army would certainly turn back to save itself. In this way, it would not only lift the siege of Zhao, but also make Wei's army exhausted. Tian Ji adopted Sun Bin's stratagem and launched an army to head straight for the girder. When Wei army heard the news, it hurriedly withdrew the troops that besieged Handan city, and marched back to rescue the girders at night. When the Wei army entered the ambush site of the Qi army, the Qi army met the Wei army earlier and earlier. Wei's army was defeated, almost completely annihilated. This is to besiege Wei in order to save Zhao, and relieve the danger facing Zhao.

In the story, when the state of Wei surrounded the state of Zhao, it did not go directly to relieve the state of Zhao, but by encircling the capital of Wei in turn, it forced him to turn around and save himself and lifted the siege that Zhao faced. The deeper meaning is: in order to solve the first thing, we find the second thing related to this thing, and we can overcome the first thing by solving this second thing.

This allusion tells us that in difficult times, we may not only rely on our own strength to win the war, but also need to unite the strength of others to win it.

This allusion can also be understood as people need to work together, that is, "divide and conquer" is not as good as "collective fighting". In the face of a fierce enemy, blindly fighting recklessly is tantamount to throwing eggs at stones. Therefore, we should avoid its sharpness, avoid the real and attack the virtual. Only under the premise of unity can we break through the dilemma and get rid of the crisis.

Whether in life or at work, the key to success is to learn to seize the opportunity and turn passivity into initiative. We should be good at finding opportunities and implementing reasonable combat strategies to maximize our own interests.

Rescuing Zhao by besieging Wei also reminds people to have the belief and determination to win, rather than passively waiting for the opportunity to come.

Successful people have a strong heart and dare to try different methods and find different paths. Only in this way can we really get rid of passivity and win.

3.Kill someone with a borrowed knife

When you do not have the means to attack your enemy directly, then attack using the strength of another. Trick an ally into attacking him, bribe an official to turn traitor, or use the enemy's own strength against him.

Get rid of your opponent by borrowing someone else's hand, but you don't show your face. This kind of indirect murder stratagem is called "killing by using the knife".

It is illegal to kill people with your own knife, and it will also bring you trouble, but you can achieve your goal by borrowing someone else's knife instead of your own. In this way, you can not be found, but also blame others in times of crisis.

In order to preserve our own strength, we should make good use of contradictions, skillfully borrow the power of the third party, break the enemy, and achieve our own goals.

If we have made it clear who the enemy is and the attitude of our allies is not clear, we should induce our allies to destroy the enemy without paying the price ourselves.

Learn to use contradictions, alienate the enemy and other Strategies, skillfully borrow the strength of other countries to defeat the enemy and save their own strength. Can be a shoo-in, greatly benefited.

If you want to achieve your goal under the circumstances that the environment is limited, you are unable or unwilling to show your face directly, you can use people and things outside yourself to achieve your goal in a planned way, so that you don't have to pay any price when you succeed; When you fail, you don't have to bear any responsibility.

Being good at using fake hands on others and skillfully borrowing external forces, you can not show any traces and show your face, so you can not bear any responsibility, which not only achieves your goals, but also leaves your hands clean.

How can we achieve the goal of "killing people by using the knife"? Borrowing someone else's knife to kill people, the owner of the knife will inevitably be lured into the partnership, and he will inevitably be involved in killing people, and naturally he will be dragged into the water. Had to be an alliance.

Borrowing and killing is a clever way to borrow words, but "borrowing" must have conditions, or state the interests, perhaps with heavy interests. The main feature of this stratagem is to weaken or eliminate the hostile potential by using the strength of the enemy or the strength of its allies. The key is to be good at capturing and benefiting the enemy's shields, including those inside the enemy and those between the enemy and its allies, and try to make these shields expand and intensify, so as to cause the enemy to compete directly or between the enemy and its allies, so as to weaken or destroy the enemy's reality.

4.Waiting at one's ease for the exhausted enemy

It is an advantage to choose the time and place for battle. In this way you know when and where the battle will take place, while your enemy does not. Encourage your enemy to expend his energy in futile quests while you conserve your strength. When he is exhausted and confused, you attack with energy and purpose.

Wait for the right opportunity comfortably and occupy the favorable situation, while preventing the enemy's attack, save your strength, and then take the initiative to attack when the enemy's morale is low. It is easy to win the fruits of victory.

"Delaware Crossing the River" in the American War of Independence. On Christmas Eve, 1776, under the command of General Washington, the continental army of the United States decided to cross the

Delaware River at night and make a surprise attack in order to avoid the pursuit of the British. After the successful raid, the American army did not directly pursue the British army, but chose to rest and reorganize its troops. They used this time to provide tired soldiers with food and rest, and at the same time strengthened the training and equipment of the army. In the end, the American continental army took advantage of the darkness and bad weather in winter night to raid the British army, captured 1000 British soldiers and won the first victory of the American War of Independence. This victory not only boosted the morale of the American army, but also made the British realize that they were not invincible.

We should not only save our strength and enhance our strength, but also keep the enemy on the run: if the enemy's power is depleted, our strength will naturally increase. First of all, we should be on the defensive, actively defend, while conserving our strength, and control the enemy according to the situation and mobilize him to run around in the preset battlefield. When the enemy is exhausted, his spirit is reduced, and the situation of the enemy and ourselves changes, he will strike after the enemy and break the enemy in one fell swoop.

First of all, we must have enough strength. When our own strength is not enough to defeat the enemy, we should avoid engaging in direct war with the enemy prematurely. Instead, we should take the initiative to retreat, seize the opportunity, and expand our strength, so that we can become stronger from weak.

When the enemy's strength is relatively strong and the momentum is fierce, in order to reduce unnecessary sacrifices, we should take the method of mobilizing the enemy to run around, so that his physical strength is exhausted and his morale is frustrated, thus weakening his strength.

Taking defense as the attack, sometimes defense is to prepare for a bigger attack, and sometimes defense itself is a special way of attack. At this time, "no war" is war, and war is no war. The so-called "told even more in silence than they had told in sound". Under special circumstances, the proactive and self-defensive stratagem of not fighting will kill the enemy's strength and morale, even better than the effect of fighting with swords and guns.

Wait for the opportunity, enter the battlefield as early as possible when the time is not ripe, have enough time to rest, make preparations before the war, and be fully familiar with the environment, so that you can grasp the initiative in the war. Strictly organize your own army, wait for the enemy's chaos, use your own calmness and wait for the enemy's impatience. This is the way to subdue the enemy psychologically. When the enemy is exhausted, sharply reduced, and the situation of the enemy and ourselves changes, seize the fighter plane and quickly mobilize troops to defeat the enemy.

To be static, to be constant, to be changeable, and to be immobile, to be reckless. Regardless of the wind and waves, sit firmly on the fishing boat. If you follow the waves, then the waves will not stop, and you will be unable to cope. Only by fishing quietly on the shore can you wait for the fish to bite.

Those who are good at fighting will inevitably avoid the enemy's strong morale and attack when the enemy is exhausted. This is the way to overwhelm the enemy from morale; Use troops close to the position to meet the enemy from afar, use rested troops to attack the exhausted enemy, and use well-fed soldiers to deal with the hungry enemy. This is the way to defeat the enemy in strength.

In the modern business field of making money by doing business, it is not an end to be willing to compromise and regress, but to win the opportunity by regress, rest and meditate, think of unexpected tricks, and benefit yourself. Because the necessary retrogression is in exchange for greater benefits, you must not blindly act and fight hard with your opponents under unfavorable business conditions. You must stop and look for opportunities, wait for opportunities, and then compete again to turn defeat into victory.

5.Plundering a burning house

When a country is beset by internal conflicts, when disease and famine ravage the population, when corruption and crime are rampant, then it will be unable to deal with an outside threat. This is the time to attack.

At the end of the 19th century, a fire broke out in China, San Francisco. American businessman John Haines took the opportunity to buy many Chinese properties that were forced to sell their properties. On the one hand, he took advantage of the chaos and predicament caused by the fire to buy properties at low prices from those who were in urgent need of funds because of the disaster. On the other hand, he also forced some residents to sell their property by threats, intimidation or taking advantage of legal loopholes. In this process, Haines took advantage of people's predicament and weak position to gain greater benefits. This act of looting while taking advantage of the fire has caused dissatisfaction and controversy among local Chinese and society.

The so-called people who rob people while taking advantage of the fire in other people's homes are in chaos, these temporary thieves. When someone else's house catches fire, they invite 10 or 20 partners to run into other people's houses and take the property when they see it. Some people take it with their hands, some carry it on their backs, and some carry it on their shoulders. When the host criticized this, they said, "I'm going to check things in my house for you." This is a hasty idea, taking advantage of people's danger to gain benefits. It's immoral to take advantage of the danger. But tactically it can be regarded as an easy way to win.

Militarily, this stratagem means that when the enemy encounters annoyance or danger, because he is too busy to cope with it, it is also the time when his defense ability is the weakest. We should make full use of this opportunity provided by the enemy to launch a sudden attack on the enemy and subdue the enemy.

The stratagem of attacking while the enemy is in danger and chaos When others are in danger, we can also see in modern social business that "taking advantage of the fire to rob" is a common tactic of business experts. In order to make their own enterprises and products invincible in the competition, both sides hope to win and try their best to compete for benefits in order to achieve the expected purpose. However, this stratagem must require you to really understand the details of your opponent, analyze and demonstrate it, and when you find that your opponent wants something from you, you can force him to accept his harsh conditions, fish in troubled waters, succeed in negotiations, and make big profits and make a fortune from it.

6.Clamour in the east, attack in the west

In any battle the element of surprise can provide an overwhelming advantage. Even when face to face with an enemy, surprise can still be employed by attacking where he least expects it. To do this you must create an expectation in the enemy's mind through the use of a feint.

Mask your real goals, by using the ruse of a fake goal, until the real goal is achieved. Tactically, this is known as an 'open feint': in front of everyone, you point west, when your goal is actually in the east.

In Aesop's fable, there is a famous story of "Clamour in the east, attack in the west", which is called "the fox and the crow". In the story, a fox tried to steal the cheese from a crow's mouth, so he praised the crow's wonderful singing with flattering words, which made the crow feel superior and proud. At this time, the crow's attention was attracted by the fox's words and began to pay attention to his own voice. The crow opened its mouth to show its voice, and the cheese fell to the ground and was taken away by the fox. The fox successfully used the stratagem of diversion to the west and achieved his goal. The fox uses a diversion stratagem to achieve his goal by guiding the other side to distract or confuse the other side.

On the battlefield, the enemy will be pinned down here and there, and the enemy will be whirled around, so that my main attack direction and true intention can be determined, so I have to be passively fortified everywhere. Time is bound to be only a parry, and if I return it, I can take advantage of the opportunity to win the victory.

On the surface, it was loud to fight the east, but in fact it attacked the west. Militarily, it refers to the surprise tactics of luring the enemy, creating an illusion for the other side and taking the opportunity to destroy the enemy. The place where we intend to fight must not be known, because then the enemy must be prepared to carry out impossible attacks in different places, and his troops will be scattered too little. Because if the enemy strengthens his front, we will weaken his rear. If he strengthens his rear, he will weaken his front.

In any battle, unexpected factors can provide an overwhelming advantage. Even face to face with the enemy, surprise can still be achieved by attacking the place where he least expects it. To do this, you must create an expectation in the enemy's mind by feinting. If you plan to attack from the right wing, you should first maneuver your left wing. If you want to invade, you should first pretend to strengthen your defense. If you plan to hold your ground, you should pack your bags.

The enemy's state of confusion and disorderly behavior, along with their lack of clear intentions, makes them vulnerable to unexpected events, similar to the overflow of water as depicted in divination. Exploiting their mental confusion and lack of direction, we can capitalize on their vulnerabilities and destroy them.

The essence of a diversion is to prematurely reveal one's true intentions. It involves diverting the enemy's attention and causing them to become careless in their defenses, allowing for a sudden and unexpected attack. By creating an illusion and pretending to be an unrelated threat, we can confuse the enemy's command structure. This provides us with an opportunity to launch a surprise assault and defeat them. There are various strategies to accomplish this, especially in offensive situations.

To ensure the success of this stratagem, it is crucial to maintain absolute confidentiality regarding our intentions and actions. This allows us to maintain the initiative and avoid falling into a passive and reactive state.

Modern enterprises also employ similar strategies. During initial negotiations, it is advisable for negotiators not to prematurely disclose the price of products. Discussing the price too early can undermine the negotiation process. Instead, it is important to first focus the conversation on the value of the products, allowing customers to fully understand their worth. Only after establishing the value should the topic of price be addressed. If discussions regarding price are necessary, it is important to frame it alongside the product's value. The key to securing the other party's commitment lies in highlighting the benefits they will receive rather than solely emphasizing the price they will pay.

7.Creating something out of nothing

You use the same feint twice. Having reacted to the first and often the second feint as well, the enemy will be hesitant to react to a third feint. Therefore the third feint is the actual attack catching your enemy with his guard down.

During the Tang Dynasty, a rebellious general named Linghu Chao besieged the city of Yongqiu. The defender of the city, Zhang Xun, devised a clever stratagem to deceive Linghu Chao's soldiers. He created over a thousand straw men, dressed them in black clothes, and lowered them from the city walls at night using ropes. Mistaking the straw men for real soldiers, Linghu Chao's soldiers shot arrows at them, unknowingly providing Zhang Xun with a large supply of arrows in just one night.

Later, during another dark night, Zhang Xun executed his stratagem further. He lowered real soldiers from the city walls while Linghu Chao's soldiers, who had been deceived before, thought they were only facing more straw men. Consequently, they stopped shooting and guarding, giving Zhang Xun a significant advantage.

Taking full advantage of the situation, Zhang Xun then lowered five hundred brave soldiers who swiftly charged into Linghu Chao's camp. They burned numerous tents and chased Linghu Chao's army for more than ten miles, causing significant disruption and chaos.

In the art of deception, creating illusions is a powerful tactic to achieve ultimate objectives. The concept of making something out of nothing revolves around not pretending to be something, but rather using deceptive means to confuse the enemy's judgment.

To blur the lines between truth and falsehood, real and fake, false information is strategically mixed with true information. This interplay of reality and deception disrupts the enemy's decision-making and actions. The purpose is to conceal the true intentions by presenting a false facade. The beauty of this stratagem lies in making it difficult for the enemy to defend against, with the key being to understand the enemy's reasoning.

By creating illusions, we can confuse the enemy and lead them astray, while simultaneously taking advantage of real movements concealed within the illusions. The truth is masked by false images, creating illusions and allowing for surprise attacks. Gradually, the false situation develops to the point where it subtly transforms into truth, without sticking to deception until the very end. Being overly deceitful is counterproductive as it is prone to being exposed and cannot be sustained. "Creating something out of nothing" refers to the transformation of deception into reality and transforming emptiness into substance. Empty illusions alone cannot defeat the enemy; only by carefully creating a false reality can we effectively overcome the enemy.

Spreading rumors, fabricating facts, and creating nonexistent entities like the fictitious Eastern region or the resurrection of the deceased are methods used to confuse the enemy and create opportunities for victory. Alternatively, blending the false with the real can make the false appear real, allowing for a subtle shift from deception to reality. By confusing the enemy and making them underestimate the situation, we gain an advantage to launch a successful attack.

In warfare, we confront the enemy face to face, requiring us to assess the present situation and demonstrate courage. Success in war relies not only on improving our own military strength but also on weakening the enemy's capabilities. This stratagem can also be applied in business to confuse opponents and achieve goals. The art of making something out of nothing involves utilizing illusions and false information to mislead opponents, gaining their belief and causing them to fall into their own traps.

The implementation of this stratagem can be divided into three steps: first, making the enemy believe it is true; second, revealing the falsehood to make the enemy underestimate the situation; and third, transforming the false into the true while the enemy still mistakes it for the false. This creates confusion in the enemy's mindset, giving us the upper hand.

The tactic of making something out of nothing, using illusions to confuse opponents, and snatching victory under the veil of deception, is frequently employed in intense market competition. It allows us to surprise opponents and achieve our real objective of financial gain.

8.Pretend to take one path while sneaking down the other

Deceive the enemy with an obvious approach that will take a very long time, while surprising him by taking a shortcut and sneak up to him. As the enemy concentrates on the decoy, he will miss you sneaking up to him.

Secretly cross Chen Cang is one of the famous historical anecdotes in China. This incident occurred in 208 BC, during a critical period when the Han army, led by Liu Bang, was facing a formidable siege by the Qin forces. In order to break through the enemy's defense, Liu Bang devised a stratagem of surprise attack.

Liu Bang assigned his trusted general, Han Xin, to lead an army. He ordered his soldiers to repair the burned plank road, creating the impression that they would attack from this route. However, this was just a diversionary tactic. In reality, Liu Bang chose a hidden opportunity during the night when the Qin forces were not on high alert. Leveraging the local terrain and road conditions, Han Xin skillfully navigated through the defense line of the Qin army. Quietly, the main force made its way along a covert path and launched an attack on a county known as Chencang.

During their march, Liu Bang implemented stringent security measures to minimize communication and noise amongst the troops, ensuring that they would not be detected by the enemy. Simultaneously, he devised a stratagem to deceive Qin Jun's investigation and surveillance by setting up fake camps and misleading marching routes. These deceptive tactics created confusion and made it difficult for the enemy to track their movements.

In the end, Liu Bang's calculated strategies paid off. He successfully led his troops to infiltrate Chencang, thereby breaking the siege imposed by Qin Jun. This victory paved the way for the establishment of the Han Dynasty.

Han Xin's "Building the plank road while Liu Bang secretly crossed the Chen Cang" is a renowned military example in Chinese history, widely discussed and admired. The key premise of this stratagem is the concept of "sneaking in" on a "clear path." This involves publicly demonstrating a seemingly harmless or foolish strategic action to make the enemy lower their guard and become complacent.

Behind this public action, there is either a real covert operation taking place or a diversion to shift the enemy's attention. By blinding the enemy with illusions and causing them to relax their vigilance, a surprise attack can be launched, resulting in a swift and decisive victory without encountering much resistance.

The success of such surprise tactics stems from adhering to fundamental principles of warfare. Without adhering to established military principles, surprise tactics will not yield favorable outcomes. In this particular case, feigning the construction of a plank road served the purpose of concealing the true intentions and positions of Liu Bang's forces.

This stratagem shares similarities with the concept of diversion, as both involve confusion and covert attacks. Feigning an attack diverts the enemy's attention and forces them to concentrate their forces on defense. However, the stratagem of hiding positions adds an additional layer of complexity. It requires deliberately planting false signs to divert attention in one direction while secretly formulating a new attack plan. By catching the enemy off guard and launching an assault when they are unprepared, victory can be achieved with little resistance.

This same stratagem can be applied in commercial warfare. For example, in order to boost sales during the holiday season, a merchant may deliberately spread a rumor that they will not participate in any price wars on Black Friday. This creates a false sense of relaxation among their competitors, confuses the competition, and allows the merchant to make significant efforts in selling their products during this period. By surprising their peers and enticing customers, the merchant can gain an advantage and win over customers.

9.Watch a fire burning from the other side of the river

Delay entering the field of battle until all the other players have become exhausted fighting amongst themselves. Then go in at full strength and pick up the pieces.

In the Spring and Autumn Period, Bian Zhuangzi, the governor of Lu, devised a plan to assassinate a tiger.However,his intention was known to his little servant, and the boy servant put forward a clever stratagem: The boy servant told Bian Zhuangzi that there were two tigers fighting for a cow nearby. He explained that when these two tigers enjoy delicious food, they are likely to fight. In this battle, the tiger with great strength may be injured, while the tiger with little strength may die.

The boy servant suggested that Bian Zhuangzi wait for the end of the fight, and then assassinate the injured tiger. In this way, Bian Zhuangzi can get two tigers in one fell swoop. Bian Zhuangzi listened to the boy's advice and waited patiently. Sure enough, in the fierce battle, the big tiger was injured. Bian Zhuangzi took the opportunity to attack and successfully assassinated the injured big tiger.

Through the clever stratagem of the boy servant, Bian Zhuangzi not only achieved his desired goal but also avoided the risk of confronting two tigers simultaneously. This story teaches us the importance of patience and timing when faced with difficulties. By observing and planning, we can find the best solution and reap greater benefits.

The concept of "sitting on the mountain and watching the tigers fight" is akin to watching a fire across the river. The correct approach is to keep a safe distance and observe as the enemy destroys themselves through infighting. This allows us to weaken and ultimately resolve the enemy's strength. However, we should not passively watch but actively design and provoke the fire to burn more violently, even taking advantage of the chaos to benefit ourselves.

Waiting for internal divisions and intensifying contradictions among the enemy forces is crucial. It is important not to engage the enemy prematurely, as it may lead to them joining together to combat a common threat. The correct approach is to remain patient and watch as they destroy each other, weakening their strength and potentially disintegrating on their own. The key characteristics of this stratagem are observation and adaptation. When the two enemy forces are locked in conflict, we should neither help nor interfere recklessly but rather wait for the situation to develop in our favor before taking action. This stratagem relies on a significant "fire" within the enemy, indicating chaos, as well as a separation, or "shore," between the conflicting parties. Without a suitable "shore," the risk of getting burned while observing the fire is high.

To stand on one side of the river and watch the fire on the other side means to stay on the sidelines when others are in danger and wait for their demise.

From a military perspective, this stratagem entails observing and exploiting the infighting between opposing forces without directly engaging in battle. By allowing their contradictions to intensify, we can benefit when both sides have suffered losses.

When seeking to attack and defeat the enemy, it is essential to avoid blindly taking advantage of the fire. Instead, we should observe, wait for the fire to develop, allow it to spread, and internally weaken the enemy's effective strength. This is the essence of watching the fire from the other side.

Once upon a time, two brothers named Yuan Shang and Yuan Xi found themselves fleeing to Liaodong with thousands of cavalry after being defeated in battle. The local satrap of Liaodong, Gongsun Kang, chose not to obey Cao Cao's commands because he believed that Cao Cao was too far away to pose a threat.

However, Cao Cao cleverly devised a stratagem after defeating the Wuhuan tribe. He suggested that Gongsun Kang should personally kill Yuan Shang and Yuan Xi and present their heads to him. In September, when Cao Cao returned with a formidable army from Liucheng, Gongsun Kang did indeed kill the Yuan brothers and handed over their heads to Cao Cao.

The other generals were puzzled by Cao Cao's stratagem and asked for an explanation. Cao Cao clarified his approach by stating, "Gongsun Kang has always feared Yuan Shang and Yuan Xi. If I were to launch an immediate attack from the outside, they would join forces against me. However, by remaining calm and passive, they ended up turning against each other. This is an objective and unavoidable situation."

This story teaches us that sometimes forceful tactics alone cannot solve problems. By leveraging others' fears and internal contradictions, we can achieve our goals in a more strategic and calculated manner.

10.Covering the dagger with a smile

Charm and ingratiate yourself with your enemy. When you have gained his trust, move against him in secret.

Note: It is essential to maintain a smiling and friendly demeanor to put others at ease, enabling them to lower their guard. However, behind this pleasant facade, you must be prepared with a secret plan to swiftly defeat the other side. This stratagem appears gentle on the surface but conceals a ruthless intention.

There was a prominent individual who outwardly appeared gentle, always wearing a smile while speaking to others. However, beneath this exterior, he was petty, suspicious, and malicious. As a person in power, he expected unwavering obedience from others, and anyone who opposed him would be framed. During that time, people referred to him as having a "knife in his smile."

The key to executing this stratagem lies in the act of smiling. Laughter must be genuine and natural, maintaining a sense of balance to make the enemy feel at ease and believe they are safe. However, excessive and contrived laughter will raise the other party's suspicions. The purpose behind the "smile" is to conceal the "knife." Regardless of the time or place, the "knife" must remain hidden within the "smile" to prevent the stratagem from being exposed. The "knife" can either be revealed or concealed, but once drawn, it must be swift and decisive, catching the enemy off guard without allowing them time to react.

In the early Qing Dynasty of China, there was a man named Wu Sangui. Originally a general of the Ming Dynasty, he surrendered to the Qing Dynasty after its downfall. However, he later rebelled against the Qing Dynasty and became a warlord in southwest China. As his power grew, he became increasingly anxious, knowing that the Qing Dynasty would inevitably seek to subdue him. To address this, he devised a stratagem. He instructed his son to surrender to the Qing Dynasty and assist in attacking him after the surrender. The stratagem succeeded, as the Qing army gradually eroded Wu Sangui's power. However, Wu Sangui seized the opportunity to eliminate the commanding officer of the Qing army and emerged victorious.

Using the stratagem of Covering the dagger with a smile, we should tailor our approach based on the characteristics of enemy commanders. For those who are arrogant, we should amplify their arrogance. Conversely, for those who are fearful, we should display sincerity and create an atmosphere that relaxes their vigilance. While appearing relaxed on the surface, we must actively prepare and seek opportunities to launch a sudden and decisive attack.

This stratagem relies on the concept of offering honey while concealing a sword. Our words should be sweeter than honey, but our intent must hold a deadly blade. We may humble ourselves and act obediently, showing apparent sincerity and adhering to others' wishes. However, underneath this facade lies a different motive, ready to take action and achieve our objectives through deceitful means.

In modern business activities, hiding a knife in a smile is also a commonly used tactic by operators. During negotiations with opponents, operators may present themselves as gentle, humble, and generous, all while wearing a smile. However, beneath this courteous demeanor, some operators may possess narrow-mindedness, an inclination for suspicion, or even sinister and vicious intentions. The purpose of this stratagem is to manipulate opponents into compliance, leading them into the trap designed by the operator, ultimately achieving their true objective of gaining wealth.

11.Sacrifice the plum for the peach

There are circumstances in which you must sacrifice short-term objectives in order to gain the long-term goal. This is the scapegoat stratagem whereby someone else suffers the consequences so that the rest do not.

In China's chess rules, Che and Shuai are two types of chess pieces. "Che" means chariot, while "Shuai" means general or commander. Originally a term used in chess, In order to keep the coach, I would rather lose the most aggressive car. This stratagem is applicable to military affairs, diplomacy, politics, economy,   and daily life. It refers to the concept of sacrificing minor resources to protect the main authority or to secure a more significant strategic advantage.

Give up what one loves reluctantly. When a gecko is caught, it will voluntarily detach its tail. Breaking its tail must be painful for the gecko, but it is a survival stratagem. Similarly, people should be willing to bear the pain and let go of things they value, just like geckos.

As for the relationship between peach trees and plum trees, plum trees can be grafted onto peach trees successfully due to their close genetic relationship. In Chinese culture, peaches and plums are used as a metaphor for the deep bond between brothers and sisters. Peach trees grow in the open courtyard, while plum trees grow next to peach trees. When insects attack the peach trees, the plum trees take their place and become the target. This metaphor highlights the idea that trees can replace each other, but sometimes, people forget the bond of brotherhood. It emphasizes the stratagem of sacrificing a smaller loss for a greater victory. It can also be interpreted as replacing one thing with another or enduring hardships for others. This stratagem involves using inferior forces to contain a superior enemy or buying time for the overall situation.

This metaphor summarizes the concept of sacrificing a part to preserve the whole in military stratagem. Military strategists often sacrifice a portion of their troops to preserve their strength and achieve ultimate victory. It is a method of adaptability and flexibility. When the situation becomes uncontrollable and losses are inevitable, one can transfer the losses or difficulties from one side to another, abandoning local interests to achieve greater gains in the overall situation. This stratagem is known as "Li Dai tao stiff."

In the late Warring States period, the northern part of Zhao was frequently attacked by the huns and other factions, causing unrest at the border. The king of Zhao decided to appoint General Li Mu to protect Yanmen Pass, a crucial gateway to the north. Upon taking office, Li Mu began rewarding his soldiers daily by killing cattle and sheep. The Huns, observing this, sent a small cavalry to plunder the livestock. Li Mu's soldiers engaged the enemy in battle and feigned retreat, deliberately leaving behind some soldiers and livestock. This tactical move was aimed at allowing the Huns to become overconfident and underestimate Li Mu's strength. The Huns took the bait and returned home victorious. Khan, the leader of the Huns, believing that Li Mu was too timid to leave the city and fight, led an army close to Yanmen Pass. However, Li Mu had anticipated this and prepared an ambush, defeating the Khan and achieving an overall victory with minimal losses.

This practice of willingly enduring suffering or sacrificing for the benefit of others has been observed throughout history. It is important to note that such actions must be conducted with moral integrity. For example, in ancient China, the warlord Cao Cao, after making a mistake, cut off his own hair rather than subject his troops to punishment. On the other hand, history, literature, and reality have also witnessed despicable acts of villains who commit crimes and blame others as scapegoats.

In the realm of business competition, achieving total victory is often challenging, and sometimes sacrifices or costs must be incurred. In these situations, it is crucial to adhere to the principle of prioritizing the greater good and minimizing harm. We should be willing to sacrifice part to safeguard the overall situation, trading short-term gains for long-term benefits, sacrificing others to save ourselves, and relinquishing small gains for larger advantages. This stratagem of forsaking the minor to protect the major involves sacrificing one side to save the other. There must be a clear connection between the two parties for this exchange to occur. It is important to understand the significance of preserving critical positions while letting go of less important ones, avoiding a narrow focus on one aspect while neglecting another, and ensuring that replacements are done in the appropriate order.

In modern business endeavors, operators should not be swayed by small profits or influenced by minor harms. Instead, they should carefully analyze and compare the overall advantages and disadvantages, strive for the primary advantages without wavering, and skillfully "retreat for progress" in order to achieve their ultimate goal of financial success.

12.picking up something in passing or Steal any passing goat
While carrying out your plans be flexible enough to take advantage of any opportunity that presents itself, however small, and avail yourself

of any profit, however slight.

A sheep is a docile animal that follows whoever is leading it. This stratagem suggests that if you finish your own tasks and happen to come across someone else's sheep along the way, you can conveniently take it back with you.

The idea behind this is to take advantage of opportunities when others are not paying attention and acquire something that would typically require more effort to obtain. It is also used to describe individuals who are quick-witted, sharp-eyed, and possess the intelligence and skills to exploit advantageous situations by taking what belongs to others.

However, it is not always necessary to bring back the "sheep" (unforeseen small gains) that you come across. First, it is important to observe whether it could be a trap or bait set by someone else to lure you in. Second, keep in mind that small profits are still small and cannot replace your main goals. Only when acquiring these small gains does not hinder the achievement of your primary objectives should you take advantage of these unexpected opportunities. Otherwise, you may lose something significant in pursuit of a minor benefit.

In military matters, there are often vulnerabilities in the enemy's mobilization process. By exploiting their negligence, you can gain advantages without engaging in regular combat. This approach applies to situations of both victory and defeat.

When stealing or seizing opportunities, it is crucial to identify weaknesses in the enemy's actions, target their vulnerable points, and implement strategies that strengthen your own position or capitalize on the situation to emerge victorious. You must have a keen eye for spotting openings and take advantage of them to reap profits. Even the smallest negligence on the part of your enemy should be capitalized upon. We must strive for any small benefits and transform the enemy's negligence into our own victories. When you identify small gaps in the enemy's defenses, you must act promptly to exploit them. If you come across small gains, you should make the effort to secure them. However, whether or not to pursue these small profits depends on the overall situation. As long as you do not "lose big because of small," you should not let go of opportunities to obtain small victories.

13.Disturb the snake by hitting the grass

Do something unarmed, but spectacular ("hitting the grass") to provoke a response of the enemy ("startle the snake"), thereby giving away his plans or position, or just taunt him.

Do something unusual, strange, and unexpected as this will arouse the enemy's suspicion and disrupt his thinking.

In mountainous villages, people often carry bamboo sticks and beat the weeds while walking, especially on paths with overgrown vegetation. Why do they do this? It is because the grassy areas are the natural habitat of venomous snakes. Many venomous snakes, such as land snakes and rattlesnakes, are small in size and have earthy-colored or grass-colored bodies. They like to hide in the grass and attack unsuspecting passersby, making it difficult to detect their presence. A snake bite can cause injuries, disabilities, and even death. However, these poisonous snakes are afraid of bamboo sticks. People mow the grass to disturb the snakes. When the snakes are scared away, it ensures the safety of pedestrians on the road.

By beating the grass around with wooden sticks, they make the snakes hiding in the grass panic and flee, thus catching them.

In the Tang Dynasty, there was a man named Wang Lu who served as a county magistrate and had the responsibility of governing the people. However, during his tenure, he engaged in corrupt practices, such as embezzlement and accepting bribes, to unlawfully acquire money, goods, and other items. His subordinates followed his lead and also demanded bribes. The people suffered greatly and bitterly complained.

One day, Wang Lu heard that his superior was coming to investigate the grievances of the people, which made him worry about the security of his position. While reviewing official documents, he accidentally came across a stack of complaints jointly filed by the county residents, denouncing his officials for accepting bribes. This heightened his anxiety, and he seemingly absentmindedly approved some characters in the complaint letter: "Even though you mow the grass, I'm still frightened like a snake in the grass." Later generations condensed this story into the idiom "spooking the snake," which means that the other party's actions were not careful enough and allowed their intentions to be noticed in advance.

In military stratagem, to understand the true intentions of the enemy, one can intentionally startle them, causing panic and revealing their true nature. Therefore, the stratagem of "startling the snake" involves using reconnaissance tactics to force the hidden opponent to disclose their true intentions. It is crucial to take action based on repeated reconnaissance and information to avoid falling into the enemy's ambush.

More widely used as "[Do not] startle the snake by hitting the grass". An imprudent act will give your position or intentions away to the enemy.

Snakes often hide in the grass, making it necessary to mow the grass in order to find them and prepare for snake hunting. If the equipment for snake hunting is not ready or the terrain is unfavorable, once the snake is discovered, you cannot effectively mow the grass to prevent the snake from escaping.

In military tactics, the concept of "scaring the snake" means that when enemy soldiers are not exposed or their intentions are unclear, one must not underestimate the enemy and rush forward. It is important to gather information about the enemy's configuration and movements before taking action.

In social life, there are often hidden intrigues and plots, much like poisonous snakes lurking in the grass. Innocent people can be hurt, and those who uphold justice can be targeted. By identifying and exposing these intrigues in advance, we can protect the innocent and upright individuals.

One effective way to uncover and expose a conspiracy is to startle the snake. Most conspirators, like thieves, have deceitful hearts. By employing strategies that bluff the conspirators while simultaneously taking precautions, we can either halt their plots or expose and take action against them.

"Startling the snake" refers to an indirect method of reconnaissance, also known as throwing stones to ask for directions, which lures the snakes out of their hiding holes. When faced with an unknown path that may contain lurking dangers, it would be risky to proceed recklessly. By mowing grass or throwing stones, the enemy will inevitably respond, potentially exposing their intentions and actions. This helps facilitate a better understanding of the situation, allowing for a stratagem of "watching and then acting" accordingly. This approach includes tactics such as firepower reconnaissance and pilot projects.

The purpose of luring the snake out of its hole is to gain knowledge about the snake's position, strength, intentions, and trends, either to avoid it or to eliminate it more easily.

"Startling the snake" also refers to an indirect method of driving. To avoid being attacked by snakes while walking, it is necessary to drive away any snakes lying on the road.

14.Borrow another's body to return the soul.

Take an institution, a technology, a method, or even an ideology that has been forgotten or discarded and appropriate it for your own purpose.

Revive something from the past by giving it a new purpose or bring to life old ideas, customs, or traditions and reinterpret them to fit your purposes.

Tie Guai Li is one of the legendary Eight Immortals in Chinese folklore, and his story is widely circulated in China. Tie Guai Li was not originally a fairy, but through long-term cultivation and practice, he gradually acquired magical abilities. The story takes place when Tie Guai Li accompanied the Taoist sage Lao Zi on a visit to Huashan Mountain. Lao Zi instructed Tie Guai Li to have an out-of-body experience in order to understand the changes of the heavens and the earth, with his physical body needing to stay in a cave. Following his master's instructions, Tie Guai Li left his body in the cave and embarked on the journey with his soul alongside Lao Zi.

However, an unexpected event occurred. Tie Guai Li's disciples had to leave temporarily due to urgent matters at home and were unable to cremate his body on time. When they returned, mistakenly believing that Tie Guai Li had passed away, they proceeded to cremate his body. Upon the return of Tie Guai Li's soul, he discovered that his body was no longer there. He then had no choice but to enter the body of a recently deceased beggar. Utilizing the beggar's body, he was able to infuse his own soul into it, thus realizing the concept of "returning the soul by borrowing the corpse". Therefore, the Tie Guai Li we know today actually possesses the body of a beggar.

This story illustrates the idea that after death, souls can attach themselves to other people's bodies and return to life, extending to the notion of something deceased being revived in some form.

Another story: In this story, a wise and courageous general confronted a powerful enemy siege and decided to utilize a clever stratagem. He discovered the body of a deceased soldier, disguised himself as the soldier, and infiltrated the enemy camp. Within the enemy camp, he clandestinely gathered information, learning about their vulnerabilities and defensive layout. Utilizing this acquired knowledge, he successfully led his troops in a surprise attack, breaking the enemy's siege. This narrative teaches us that, at times, we must employ cunning means and strategies, feigning weakness or disguising ourselves outwardly, in order to achieve unforeseen outcomes.

This concept can be applied to various situations. It suggests that rather than employing methods that are visibly strong and vital, it can be advantageous to utilize elements that are perceived as decadent or obsolete, as they may possess hidden potential. It does not imply being dominated by others, but rather assuming control over others.

In human society, the practice of achieving personal goals under the guise of others is widespread. During times of political change, some individuals may position themselves as supporters of fallen monarchs, not with the genuine intention of restoring the previous regime, but as a means to manipulate public sentiment and pursue their own political ambitions in the quest for power. Even during periods of relative stability, careerists can manipulate a ruler who may be their puppet, using their influence and control to shape state affairs. Those who lend military power to others, or act in place of others in attacking or defending, can be seen as metaphorically "borrowing the soul" of luck.

On a positive note, this concept can also be understood as the ability to rise again after falling, seeking opportunities for a comeback. When faced with failure, maintaining a clear mind, analyzing the situation calmly, making accurate judgments, and sparing no effort to seek alternatives can lead to turning defeat into victory, rather than succumbing to despair and accepting permanent defeat.

Additionally, there are instances in which external assistance aids in achieving harmony. When sheer numbers alone are insufficient to turn the tide, it becomes necessary to rely on quality over quantity, seeking strategic alliances and advantageous partnerships to bolster one's chances of success. By implementing plans under different circumstances, the ultimate objective can be accomplished without attracting undue attention.

The general principle of borrowing from the outside suggests that it is preferable to borrow from those who are capable but passive, as it allows for easier manipulation and control without arousing suspicion from others. Avoiding those who are both capable and active ensures a higher level of dominance and influence.

15.Luring the tiger out of his den

Never directly attack an opponent whose advantage is derived from its position. Instead lure him away from his position thus separating him from his source of strength.

The tiger, being the king of the mountain, must first be lured out of its territory in order to capture it easily. This metaphor implies that by employing strategical methods, one can entice the enemy to relinquish their advantageous position and exploit an opportunity to attack.

When the tiger strays from its mountainous domain, it loses its prestige. Similarly, a formidable adversary who vacates their stronghold and forfeits their advantage will engage in a decisive battle without any favorable conditions. By exploiting unfavorable weather conditions and enticing the enemy with artificial illusions, we can create a disturbance and divert their attention.

When the enemy occupies a fortified or challenging position, we can discontinue the attack and wait for a more opportune moment. In military terms, if the enemy is strong and entrenched, and if natural barriers impede progress, it is futile to launch a direct assault. Therefore, the optimal stratagem is to lure the powerful enemy away from their stronghold and then annihilate them.

Throughout history, various factions and power groups have continuously established sites or spheres of influence as arenas for competition and conflict. Luring the tiger out of the mountain has always been a commonly used method for one faction to eliminate or weaken another. Through this approach, the most critical, important, or dangerous opponent is led out of their territory, depriving them of the protective barriers of resistance.

In both ancient and modern warfare, both in China and abroad, numerous examples exist of employing this stratagem to mobilize the enemy to abandon their favorable terrain and subsequently defeat them. Moreover, this stratagem finds extensive application in modern politics, diplomacy, economics, and other fields, often yielding unforeseen results.

One notable historical instance of "diverting the tiger from the mountain" is the Russian military action in Crimea during the Ukrainian crisis in 2014. Given the complexities of geopolitics and the involvement of multiple global powers such as Russia, Ukraine, Europe, and the United States, Russia employed a stratagem that appeared as "diverting the tiger from the mountain" to external observers. Initially, Russia deployed military forces in Crimea and subsequently announced its annexation into Russian territory. This caught Europe, America, and other nations off guard, as they had originally intended to contain Russia's influence in Ukraine through economic sanctions. However, the sudden Crimea issue disrupted their plans and forced them to readjust their strategies.

This story exemplifies the essence of the stratagem of "diverting the tiger from the mountain." When faced with formidable opponents or difficulties, skillfully luring the adversary away from their favorable terrain or original defensive line enables smooth action and the acquisition of an advantage.

In modern business activities, when competing for a market with an opponent and negotiation fails, one can consider attacking the opponent's alternative market. This diversionary tactic forces the opponent to split their attention between the two fronts, making it difficult to allocate sufficient resources to both. Consequently, the opponent may be compelled to make concessions, ultimately leading to one's own success.

16.Letting the enemy off in order to catch him

Cornered prey will often mount a final desperate attack. To prevent this you let the enemy believe he still has a chance for freedom.

His will to fight is thus dampened by his desire to escape. When in the end the freedom is proven a falsehood the enemy's morale will be defeated and he will surrender without a fight.

In Aesop's Fables, there is a story called "The Lion and the Mouse." In this story, a little mouse accidentally encounters a lion, who could have easily killed it. However, unexpectedly, the lion chose to let the mouse go. Deeply grateful, the mouse promised to repay the lion if the opportunity arose in the future. Shortly after, the lion becomes trapped in a hunter's net. Desperate, the little mouse gnaws through the net rope and sets the lion free. This story vividly illustrates the stratagem of "playing hard to get," where one allows the opponent to go first and anticipates possible reciprocity in the future.

In a Chinese story, during the Three Kingdoms period, there was a prominent figure named Zhuge Liang from the Shu Kingdom. He captured Meng Huo, a tribal leader in southern China, seven times, and each time, he released him. This story exemplifies the concept that mutual captures and releases are necessary before capturing and convincing the other party. In the first six captures, Zhuge Liang physically restrained Meng Huo, but his spirit remained unconvinced. Only by killing Meng Huo would his rebellion cease. However, by the seventh capture, Meng Huo's heart was completely won over, and he became willing to submit, vowing not to resist any longer. The Shu Kingdom consolidated its control over the south as a result. Therefore, the seven instances of capture and release were not a waste of soldiers' lives, but rather a strategic approach that convinced the other side through repeated capture and release.

In order to strategically handle the situation, there are certain tactics that need to be employed. When aiming for convergence, we must initially adopt an expansionist approach. If the intention is to weaken something, it must be temporarily strengthened. If the stratagem is to abandon it, it must be temporarily elevated. And if the goal is to acquire it, it must be temporarily surrendered.

Engaging in deliberate indulgence towards the enemy during an encircling attack is not an arbitrary act of leniency, but rather a method of initially loosening the pressure so as not to push the enemy too hard. Coercion implies that soldiers will resist and the situation will deteriorate rapidly if excessive force is applied. Instead of pressuring relentlessly, it is more effective to tire out their strength, disperse them, and then capture them without much bloodshed.

Applying direct pressure on the enemy will provoke violent counterattacks. Avoiding direct confrontation, however, naturally reduces the enemy's power. This doesn't mean we shouldn't pursue the enemy, but rather we should carefully consider how to pursue them. If we drive the enemy into a corner, they will be forced to concentrate their efforts and fight back desperately. It is more advantageous to relax for a while, allowing the enemy to lower their guard and loosen their will, and then seize an opportunity to annihilate them.

Since we cannot afford to let the enemy go, we should refrain from confronting them head-on. This weakens their physical strength while allowing us to understand their intentions. By waiting for the enemy to exhaust their true strength, we can conquer them without wasting unnecessary time.

We should capture the enemy when they become tired of fleeing. As long as the enemy in our grasp believes there is even the slightest chance of escape, they will desperately try to run away. Fleeing in panic not only consumes physical energy but also wears down their mental fortitude. By presenting them with the threat of death while leaving them with the illusion of escape, they will exert all their effort to avoid harm. Their physical and mental capacities are limited, and when they tire from running, they will stop. At this point, they will lose their resistance, offering us an opportunity to capture or overcome them. If we fail to seize them when they grow weary of fleeing and they still possess the capacity to resist, they will likely fight to the death. In such a scenario, violent counterattacks by the enemy are inevitable, resulting in significant losses.

17.Bait a piece of jade with a brick

Bait someone by making him believe he gains something or just make him react to it ("toss out a brick") and obtain something valuable from him in return ("get a jade gem").

Fishing requires bait, and the fish will only take the bait when they taste its sweetness. "Brick" and "jade" are figurative metaphors.

"Jade" symbolizes victory in combat and refers to valuable speech or exquisite works. It represents success and high-quality output.

On the other hand, "brick" refers to profit and serves as bait. Metaphorically, it represents superficial knowledge or poor work.

To throw bricks means to use worthless bricks to attract extremely precious jade. It involves using something of little value in exchange for valuable strategies. The concept is about starting small and being able to grow and transform into something significant, as well as turning cheap things into valuable ones.

The "introduction" is the right path, and "brick-throwing" is a stratagem employed to achieve it. This stratagem is akin to confusing and deceiving the enemy in order to trap them and then take the opportunity to defeat them.

When the enemy seizes an advantage, they will fall into the trap and suffer. In military stratagem, it is often said that offering the enemy a small benefit willingly can make them take the bait, ultimately leading to a big victory. There have been many successful cases throughout China's history.

One example is the Kingdom of Chu, which employed old, weak, and disabled soldiers to lure enemy soldiers into attacking, and then defeated them and compelled them to sign a treaty. Additionally, the leader of the huns tribe once gave the Taihu tribe their finest horses and beauties, inducing the Taihu tribe to become lax in their defenses, ultimately leading to the assimilation of the Taihu tribe and the unification of the entire huns.

From these historical examples, we can extract valuable lessons for life. Taking a small lead can lead to a significant advantage. By giving something small to others, we may receive something much bigger in return. We start by presenting smaller, more general things as a demonstration and suggestion, purposefully inducing the other party to offer larger and more valuable things. This method of using one thing to drive or induce another is known as the "attraction of big things with small ones."

In addition to attracting more with small actions, we can also achieve more with fewer resources. By demonstrating our capabilities or ideas (represented by bricks), we can lead others to follow suit (represented by jade), and so on.

18.Capturing the ringleader first in order to capture all the followers

If the enemy's army is strong but is allied to the commander only by money, superstition or threats, then take aim at the leader.

If the commander falls the rest of the army will disperse or come over to your side.

If, however, they are allied to the leader through loyalty then beware, the army can continue to fight on after his death out of vengeance.

Boxers should wear helmets for head protection, and ball players should wear knee pads to safeguard their knees. These vulnerable parts are essential for athletes to protect to avoid injuries. Similarly, when defending against an enemy, it is crucial to prioritize and focus on safeguarding the "core parts" to prevent being captured.

The concept of a "paralysis attack" proposed by British military scientist Fuller refers to disabling the enemy's ability to organize and command the battle by targeting their command system.

The "Five Rings Theory" put forward by Colonel Wharton of the US Air Force identifies the "leadership ring" as the primary target to strike hard at the beginning of a war. In operations such as "decapitation," the target is usually influential enemy individuals, including senior commanders and local politicians.

When dealing with different tasks, it is important to utilize appropriate tools or techniques. Skilled archers should use strong bows and long arrows for maximum effectiveness. If the objective is to shoot people, targeting their mounts (horses or vehicles) first is paramount. If the aim is to catch a thief, apprehending the leader of the thieves is essential. There is a folk saying that "it takes seven inches to hit a snake," which implies targeting the snake's fatal spot, its heart, for an effective strike. By striking at the heart, the snake will naturally perish. Otherwise, even if the snake is severed into two parts, it can still pose a threat.

In battle, the enemy's main force and its leaders should be neutralized initially to fragment their fighting capability. The term "Wang" refers to the leader or chief. By capturing the leader first, when dealing with thieves, grasping the key figure among them is essential. This means taking control of the primary elements first and capturing or neutralizing the main characters. In military terms, it refers to destroying the enemy's main force or commander first to influence and weaken the entire enemy army, leading to their ultimate defeat.

This approach aims to quickly dismantle the enemy by eliminating their main force, capturing their leader, and causing their complete disintegration. Strategically, capturing the thief king means swiftly destroying the enemy by eliminating their leader and dismantling their headquarters. Achieving victory does not merely entail defeating the enemy; it requires neutralizing their backbone. Allowing the thief king to escape is akin to letting a tiger return to the mountains. However, capturing the thief king can lead the enemy into a state of leaderless and internal chaos.

Therefore, when dealing with problems, it is vital to address the key points and crucial aspects. By focusing on the core issues, we can achieve efficient and effective results. In the context of destroying and disintegrating an organization, the primary target of attack is their leaders and core figures. Once these key individuals are removed, the organization will be left leaderless.

Capturing the king represents the primary and core objective in controlling and dismantling an organization. While direct capture or forceful elimination is one approach, it often comes with high costs and challenges to succeed.

19.Take away the firewood under the cooking pot

Take out the leading argument or asset of someone; "steal someone's thunder". This is the very essence of indirect approach: instead of attacking enemy's fighting forces, the attacks are directed against his ability to wage war.

To stop boiling water in a pot, you can achieve this by placing firewood under the pot. Boiling and cold water are common occurrences in daily life. To make the water in the pot boil, you need to light a fire at the bottom of the pot and add firewood. Conversely, if you want to prevent the water from boiling, you can add cold water to the pot or remove the firewood from beneath it. These actions represent drastic measures. However, it is important to note that even if the boiling subsides momentarily when cold water is added, the water will eventually boil again. This does not provide a permanent solution.

The key lies in addressing the situation at the bottom of the pot. Water boils because of the fire underneath, and the fire requires fuel. By fundamentally eliminating the basis or dependence of water boiling, you can effectively stop the boiling process.

In both ancient and modern warfare, logistics support, particularly the provision of grain and supplies, serves as the foundation for troop survival and combat effectiveness. Thus, the saying "the soldiers and horses have not moved, and the grain and grass come first" holds true. When Cao Cao faced Yuan Shao in a direct confrontation, he realized that he might not be able to defeat Yuan Shao's forces head-on. To overcome this challenge, Cao Cao devised a clever stratagem. He burned down Yuan Shao's grain depots and cut off his supply lines, leading to a significant defeat of Yuan Shao's army.

During the Eastern Han Dynasty, there was a military officer named Wu Han who was appointed as a secretary. Once, when the enemy launched a night attack on the military camp, the soldiers in the camp panicked. However, Wu Han remained calm and composed, lying in bed without showing any signs of panic. When the soldiers heard of Wu Han's calmness, their own emotions stabilized, and the camp became quiet. Seizing this opportunity, Wu Han selected elite and brave soldiers to counterattack overnight, driving the enemy into retreat. This was not a direct resistance against the enemy's fierce momentum, but rather a stratagem to eliminate the root cause of their attack.

To solve a problem, it is essential to address it at its root. In military affairs, this often involves cutting off the enemy's supply sources, destroying the conditions on which the enemy relies, or disintegrating their morale. When the enemy possesses overwhelming strength and direct confrontation is not feasible, it is important to use strategies to weaken their momentum, yielding to them initially, and then exploiting their weaknesses. In love, the battlefield, shopping malls, or the political arena, there are countless ways to win the battle. When direct confrontation is impossible, it is necessary to weaken the root cause of the enemy's strength or disrupt their advantageous position.

By doing so, the problem can be solved effectively and tactfully.

20.Muddling the water to catch the fish; fishing in troubled waters

Create confusion and use this confusion to further your own goals.

"Muddying the water" or "fishing in troubled waters" is a convenient method for catching fish. By muddying the water, the energy of the fish is reduced, making it harder for them to distinguish what is real and what is not. This increases the chances of catching the fish by chance.

In Aesop's Fables, a collection of stories by the Greek fable writer in the 6th century BC, there is a tale about fishing in troubled waters. In this story, a fisherman fishing in a river stops the flow of water to build a net and then strikes the bottom of the water with a rope tied to a stone. This causes the fish to swim in fear, with some crashing into the net. Some local people criticize the fisherman for muddying the water and making it undrinkable. However, the fisherman responds by saying that if he hadn't muddied the water, he wouldn't have caught any fish, and without fish, he would have starved. The skill of catching fish is to be adept at fishing in troubled waters.

This metaphor illustrates the idea of taking advantage of chaotic situations to benefit oneself. In military terms, it refers to seizing opportunities during chaotic attacks to defeat weaker enemies who are still indecisive. By capitalizing on the confusion within the enemy's ranks, one can exploit their weaknesses and gain followers.

In the business world, some individuals excel in employing a "scrambled egg tactic" to fish in troubled waters. This tactic involves deliberately confusing and exhausting the other party, making simple negotiations unnecessarily complicated. Taking advantage of the other party's weariness, they forcefully push their own agenda.

The key to success in stirring things up lies in creating confusion, rendering others unable to make clear comparisons for some time. In a turbulent environment, various elements get mixed up in the chaotic vortex. To seize the opportunity for expansion, one must exploit the moment when those who are temporarily undecided and wavering are uncertain. This stratagem allows them to gain benefits by taking advantage of the confusion.

Profiting from chaos or taking advantage of chaotic situations to reap benefits is one of the many methods employed in competitive environments. The stock market, for example, occasionally presents a turbulent and chaotic environment. By emulating the strategies of predators like Warren E.Buffett and George Soros, one can become skilled at seizing opportunities and avoid missing out on advantageous situations.

However, it's worth noting that fishing in troubled waters is sometimes recognized and seen through. An example from the Warring States Period involves a monarch from the State of Qi who enjoyed listening to music ensembles. He formed a band consisting of experts recommended to him. Mr. Nan Guo, who couldn't play the flute, was misleadingly endorsed as highly skilled and included in the band by King Qi Xuan. He sat among a band of 300 people pretending to play the cymbals, but in reality, he made no sound. For many years, he received the same high salary as other musicians. However, when the son of the king ascended to the throne and developed a preference for solo music, Mr. Nan Guo couldn't fish in troubled waters anymore out of fear of being discovered. He resorted to boasting and establishing a false reputation in order to conceal his lack of talent.

21.getting away like the cicada sloughing its skin; Slipping away by casting off a cloak;

Mask yourself. Either leave one's distinctive traits behind, thus becoming inconspicuous, or masquerade as something or someone else.

This stratagem is mainly used to escape from enemy of superior strength.

After a dormant period, cicadas emerge from the ground with bright yellow bodies, earning them the nickname "golden cicadas." They climb up tree trunks or branches and rest quietly as they undergo a transformation. When a cicada reaches adulthood, it must shed its larval shell. There is a crack in the back of the golden shell, and the new cicada crawls out of it and flies away once its wings are fully developed. The empty golden shell remains on the branches, swaying in the wind. Unless you look closely, you wouldn't know that the new cicada has flown away. This process is known as the "golden cicada shedding its shell."

Humans have adopted the metaphor of the golden cicada shedding its shell as a means of escape, which can be found in various historical and literary works. For instance, when Gongziyuan retreated from the State of Zheng, he carefully planned his escape to avoid pursuit. He left the camp intact and the flag untouched, slipping out of the territory of Zheng unnoticed at night, just like a skilled golden cicada shedding its shell.

In the story of the Water Margin, towards the end of the Song Dynasty, the hero Song Jiang led a group of 108 people to occupy the Liangshan Marsh. They engaged in pillaging the homes of the rich to help the poor. In this tale, after Song Jiang and other leaders were captured, they devised a stratagem to escape. They had some individuals pretend to be the leaders and stay in the Liangshan Marsh while the real leaders took the opportunity to flee. The trick was to find someone to act as their body double, essentially becoming a "golden cicada."

Using the term "golden cicada" in a metaphorical sense refers to a person attempting to escape a situation at a critical moment. By leaving behind various disguises and creating the illusion that one has not left, they have actually escaped. This double strategies or escape stratagem is executed by leaving a superficial deception, making it difficult for others to immediately perceive the truth. This applies not only metaphorically, but also militarily, where it refers to the stratagem of deceiving the enemy by secretly transferring forces and launching a surprise attack elsewhere. "The golden cicada sheds its shell" signifies the tactic of maintaining a motionless appearance with military forces to lower the enemy's guard, while secretly moving the main military forces.

At this critical juncture, the aim is to create a fake image and then secretly escape, effectively hiding from the enemy. This clever method of escape is like shedding a shell. "Shedding the shell" is not a meaningless act but a strategic separation tactic. After the transfer of forces, the original position must continue to display flags, banners, and maintain the previous lineup and momentum convincingly. This ensures that the enemy is hesitant to act and friendly forces do not suspect anything. Only when they return after defeating the enemy elsewhere do the friendly and enemy forces realize the truth (or they may not even realize it at all). "The cicada sheds its shell" is an ingenious stratagem to secretly deploy skilled warriors to attack the enemy in another location while engaged in battle.

This stratagem is employed when there is a significant power imbalance, and one finds themselves in a passive, disadvantageous situation. It allows for a quick escape from the enemy and a smooth transfer or retreat. To avoid being detected or pursued by the enemy, a false appearance is left behind to deceive and stabilize them while ensuring a safe getaway. This stratagem demonstrates an active retreat, giving the impression that one is not leaving. It is crucial to choose the right timing to implement this stratagem.

On one hand, "shedding the shell" should not occur prematurely. As long as there is a possibility of victory, one should continue the fight. "Shedding the shell" should only occur when necessary. On the other hand, it is also important not to delay too long. In the event of an inevitable defeat, staying even for one more minute increases the risks and reduces the chances of survival.

getting away like the cicada sloughing its skin represents a proactive retreat and transfer, conducted in a critical situation where even a slight mistake may result in disaster. It is essential to calmly observe and analyze the situation before taking decisive action.

22.Catching the thief by closing / blocking his escape route

To capture your enemy, or more generally in fighting wars, to deliver the final blow to your enemy, you must plan prudently if you want to succeed. Do not rush into action.

Before you "move in for the kill", first cut off your enemy's escape routes, and cut off any routes through which outside help can reach them.

"Closing the door to catch thieves" is a well-known stratagem from ancient China. During the Warring States Period, when Qin attacked

Zhao, General Lian Po of Zhao chose to hold his ground and avoid direct confrontation with Qin Jun. Fan Sui, an advisor to the King of Qin, took advantage of this and planted suspicion about Lian Po in the mind of the Prince of Zhao. As a result, Zhao Kuo was sent to replace Lian Po and adopt a different stratagem, engaging in frequent face-to-face battles with Qin Jun. This change in stratagem allowed Qin Jun to exploit Zhao Kuo's underestimation of the enemy and deliberately let him win a few small victories, further inflating his confidence. Eventually, Zhao Kuo fell into Qin Jun's trap and suffered heavy losses.

The concept of "closing the door to catch thieves" stems from the idea of trapping thieves by sealing off any means of escape and then apprehending them, much like catching a turtle in a jar. When a crafty thief enters a house to steal, one must close all the doors and windows to prevent their escape, thereby capturing them and recovering the stolen goods. The reason for closing the door while catching a thief is not only to prevent their escape but also to protect them from being aided by others. Moreover, once the thief has escaped, pursuing them again may lead to falling into their trap.

In practical application, "closing the door to catch thieves" refers to the stratagem of surrounding and eliminating weak enemy forces. Allowing the enemy to escape complicates the situation and can result in a desperate counterattack or falling into the enemy's trap. This stratagem emphasizes the importance of containment and control in order to destroy the enemy.

In military terms, the term "thief" refers to enemies who are cunning, adept at surprise attacks, and elusive. Militarily, it denotes the stratagem of encircling and annihilating small, treacherous enemy groups. When dealing with such groups, the focus should be on besieging and destroying them. If they are allowed to escape, it will be highly disadvantageous for pursuers.

There are various ways to implement the "closing the door to catch thieves" stratagem. One common approach is to set up a bag-shaped formation, blocking the enemy's retreat and closing the mouth of the bag once they enter it. Another method is to tightly encircle the enemy's compound, denying them any chance of escape and annihilating them. However, regardless of the technique used, two factors should be considered: the location of the "closed door" should facilitate the total annihilation of the enemy while allowing for the concentration of superior forces. Seizing the opportune moment is crucial for success. Timing is especially important, as this stratagem is primarily applicable to weaker enemy forces and not stronger opponents. Surrounding a strong enemy with a "house" would likely result in the door being broken and the stratagem failing. Generally, this stratagem is used against weaker enemies or weak forces. After "closing the door," it is imperative to guard the exit to prevent the enemy from fleeing. The "thief" trapped within the "house" will not passively accept capture but will fight fiercely to break out of the tight encirclement. Therefore, keeping the door secure is of utmost importance.

23.Befriending the distant enemy while attacking a nearby enemy

It is known that nations that border each other become enemies while nations separated by distance and obstacles make better allies.

When you are the strongest in one field, your greatest threat is from the second strongest in your field, not the strongest from another field.

To clarify the meaning of the stratagem, let us first examine a story:

Fan Ju, a native of Wei, went to the State of Qin to persuade them and met King Zhao of Qin. King Zhao asked Fan Ju about the stratagem of attacking the fortified state. Fan Ju looked and said, "Currently, the most powerful of the seven states is Qin. Unifying the entire country should be effortless. We should first eliminate the immediate threats and then gradually expand outward." Following Fan Sui's advice, King Zhao retracted his troops that were prepared to attack the distant state of Qi and instead turned to attack the neighboring state of Wei. As a result, Qin was able to seize a large amount of land from neighboring countries, thus laying a solid foundation for Qin Shihuang's unification of China.

In essence, "Befriending the distant enemy while attacking a nearby enemy" refers to a stratagem of creating and utilizing divisions, disintegrating enemy alliances, and implementing a divide-and-conquer approach. Its key principle is that when achieving military objectives becomes difficult due to geographical constraints, one should first target the nearest enemy and refrain from engaging distant enemies. The purpose is to prevent the formation of enemy alliances and to divide and conquer them one by one. The stratagem of "making friends with distant enemies" serves to avoid excessive diplomatic deception and the creation of too many enemies.

The stratagem of "Befriending the distant enemy while attacking a nearby enemy" is based on the idea of exploiting contradictions, dividing and disintegrating enemy alliances, and utilizing a divide-and-conquer stratagem. Its technique lies in recognizing that attacking nearby enemies is beneficial, while attacking distant enemies is detrimental when limited by geography and circumstances.

Each enemy possesses different geographical locations, objectives, values, and perceptions of danger. Thus, they have different approaches to reaching us. As a result, we cannot generalize our actions but instead must tailor our responses based on their unique circumstances. By adopting varying stratagem against different enemies, we effectively divide them.

No matter how powerful an enemy may be, it becomes challenging for them to withstand the combined efforts of multiple enemies. Under such circumstances, it is advantageous to pre-emptively divide and break the alliance between them, rendering them passive and unable to cooperate. When enemies cannot cooperate or aid one another, it becomes easier to defeat them. The key is to concentrate on dealing with the immediate enemy and isolate them. It is important to note that "distant friendship" does not imply long-term reconciliation. A distant enemy remains an enemy, and sooner or later they become a confidant. Thus, considering distant enemies is merely a temporary diplomatic stratagem to avoid creating an excessive number of enemies. Once the nearby enemy is conquered, the purpose of the temporary friendship with the distant enemy is fulfilled.

When facing an enemy alliance composed of multiple enemies, it is essential to divide and disintegrate them, ensuring they do not unite against us. If we have good relations with neighboring countries, it can lead to confusion and chaos. By prioritizing friendship with distant enemies, we prevent distractions and utilize a divide-and-conquer approach to systematically defeat nearby enemies.

Inbreeding comes with two disadvantages. It is akin to sleeping next to a snoring couch. Even if the nearby enemy is temporarily calmed, they can turn against us at any moment. The close enemy is in our vicinity, binding us tightly and limiting our outward development. To continue expanding, we must overcome this obstacle. On the other hand, there are three disadvantages to far attacks. They are costly, as they involve long-distance operations that may be less effective than targeting nearby enemies.

24. Obtain safe passage to conquer the enemy

Borrow the resources of an ally to attack a common enemy. Once the enemy is defeated, use those resources to turn on the ally that lent you them in the first place.

A donkey carrying heavy goods gasped and asked a horse, who carried only a small amount of goods, for help: "Can you help me carry some of my load? It's nothing for you, but it would relieve me of a lot of burden."

The horse replied unhappily, "Why should I help you carry your things? I'm happy with my light load!"

Soon after, the donkey died from exhaustion. The owner then added all the donkey's goods to the horse's load, and the horse regretted its decision.

This story teaches us that when someone around us encounters difficulties, we should extend a helping hand and assist them in overcoming their challenges. Only then will they be grateful to us and willing to repay our kindness in the future.

When a small country is caught between two major powers, and one of them threatens to subjugate it, the other should immediately send troops to assist in order to expand their influence.

For instance, during the Spring and Autumn Period, the State of Jin's borrowed the road through the State of Yu to attack the State of Guo. As a result, the State of Guo was defeated and fled to Luoyang, the capital of the Zhou Dynasty. After destroying the State of Guo, the Jin's army, on its way back, once again borrowed the road through the State of Yu and launched an attack while their guard was down, ultimately destroying the State of Yu.

This stratagem involves using the roads of other countries to launch covert and unexpected attacks on the enemy. In military terms, it often entails bypassing a middle area and first attacking a distant enemy, then turning back to destroy them after isolation. China may send troops to rescue a country located between the enemy and our own, utilizing the opportunity to expand our influence. However, a country in such a situation may find it difficult to trust our intentions if we solely take action.

Related strategies include "kick down the bridge after crossing the river" and "kill two birds with one stone." It is akin to crossing a river by borrowing a bridge from home, only to destroy the bridge once we have crossed. The State of Jin successfully captured the State of Guo under the pretense of borrowing the road through the State of Yu. This caused the State of Yu to lower its guard, lose its source of rescue, and subsequently be easily defeated by the Jin's army on their return. Achieving victory over two countries with a single military operation can truly be described as killing two birds with one stone and gaining substantial advantages.

It is comparable to crossing a river using a borrowed boat or bridge. In situations where we lack a bridge, we can use a boat to reach the other side. However, there is apprehension that using someone else's boat may result in damage or significant cost. Thus, a favorable condition for borrowing a boat is to have a convincing and justifiable reason, which can convince the boat owner to willingly lend it. This ensures a smooth journey to the other side without incurring any costs or paying a high price.

An additional story that illustrates this concept is about repaying debts with animosity. During the Tang Dynasty, there was a county commandant named Li Mian who once released a prisoner. Many years later, they encountered each other in a foreign land. The former prisoner invited his benefactor to his home and asked his wife how to repay the favor. His wife suggested killing him. The initial convenience provided to one another now became a hidden danger.

25.Stealing the beams and pillars and replacing them with rotten timbers

Disrupt the enemy's formations, interfere with their methods of operations, change the rules in which they are used to following, go contrary to their standard training.

In this way you remove the supporting pillar, the common link that makes a group of men an effective fighting force.

Beams and columns are crucial components of building structures, providing stability and support. They are typically made of thick, strong, and straight materials such as wood. The stability of a building relies heavily on the integrity of its beams and columns. If the beams are weak, the structure may collapse, and if the columns fail, it can also lead to a collapse.

According to legend, during the Spring and Autumn Period in ancient China, the ruler of the State of Jin's desired to construct a tall palace.

The carpenter in charge of the construction saw a high-quality, large pillar and decided to steal it for his own use. Over a period of time, the carpenter secretly stole one big and long pillar from the palace each night and replaced it with shorter beams. Once the palace was completed, the carpenter collected his reward, sold the stolen pillars, and fled with the ill-gotten gains. Shortly after completion, a strong wind blew and the palace collapsed. When the ruler investigated the matter and went looking for the carpenter, he found the carpenter's house empty.

This story has led to the proverb "stealing the beam to replace the column," which metaphorically signifies the act of improperly substituting essential parts of things to achieve personal goals, thereby altering the nature and essence of the original object.

Here's another example:In a scenario of a criminal serving a life sentence, he bribes the corrupt guard Jack to help him escape. Jack finds a young man who closely resembles the criminal and convinces him to take the criminal's place in prison. Using chaos and laxity as cover, they conspire to switch identities and escape. The next morning, the prison authorities discover that the criminal serving a life sentence has vanished, leaving behind the innocent young man who was imprisoned for a minor crime. The criminals successfully switched identities and escaped from the prison.

In the case of Samson from the Bible, he was a renowned judge and mighty warrior of Israel. Samson possessed great strength and once killed a lion with his bare hands. The Philistines, seeking to defeat him, used Delilah, a beautiful woman, to seduce him and discover the source of his strength - his hair. While Samson was sleeping, they shaved off his hair and captured him. Samson became a slave, enduring suffering but eventually regained his strength. In the enemy's temple, with both hands, Samson pushed and brought down a large column, causing the temple to collapse, leading to mutual destruction with his enemies. This story further emphasizes the significance of beams and columns in the survival of structures.

Given the critical role that beams and columns play in building construction, it is crucial to protect them from individuals with ulterior motives who may compromise their quality or replace them with inferior substitutes.

26. Reviling / abusing the locust tree while pointing to the mulberry

To discipline, control, or warn others whose status or position excludes them from direct confrontation; use analogy and innuendo. Without directly naming names, those accused cannot retaliate without revealing their complicity.

"abusing the locust tree while pointing to the mulberry" is a metaphorical expression used to scold or criticize someone indirectly, without engaging in direct conflict. This technique allows individuals to vent their emotions and express their dissatisfaction without directly confronting the person in question.

This metaphorical expression implies that when someone wants to scold another person but finds it inconvenient or inappropriate to do so directly, they choose to criticize a different object or individual. By doing this, the intended target of the scolding understands that they are the real subject of the criticism, even though they are not explicitly named and cannot retaliate.

There are numerous anecdotes in Chinese culture that revolve around the practice of criticizing mulberry trees to indirectly scold someone. These anecdotes serve as examples of this metaphorical approach used in various situations.

In many Chinese families, it is common for multiple generations to live together in one household. During mealtimes, dishes are placed on the table to demonstrate care and warm hospitality towards family members. This tradition reflects the importance of family unity and the expression of concern for one another.

In this heartwarming story, there is an 80-year-old father, his son, and his daughter-in-law, all in their fifties, along with their university-age grandchildren. During the summer vacation, their young grandson came home, bringing joy to the family. The son and daughter-in-law were thrilled and prepared a special dinner, including chickens and ducks, to celebrate their son's return. During the meal, the son and daughter-in-law focused their attention on their grandson, offering him chicken legs and duck breast, while inadvertently neglecting the old father.

Feeling left out, the old father took matters into his own hands and put a chicken leg in his son's bowl, saying, "Son, eat." Surprised by this gesture, the son remarked, "I am already over 50 years old, do you still want to feed me?" The old father smiled warmly and replied, "You may feel sorry for your son, but can't I also feel sorry for my son?"

Upon hearing his father's words, the son realized that he had not been attentive enough to his father's needs and felt ashamed of his neglect. The old father chose not to directly point out his son's lack of filial piety but instead expressed his concern through this simple act of adding food to his son's bowl, hoping to kindle a sense of reflection within him.

There is a story called "Kill the chicken for the monkey."

Monkeys are known to be stubborn animals that often resist training. In an acrobatic troupe, the monkey trainer faced difficulties in taming a particular monkey. To find a solution, the trainer devised a clever stratagem. He killed a chicken in front of the monkey, using the shocking and horrifying sight to intimidate and control the monkey. This stratagem effectively tamed the monkey, who subsequently performed acrobatics on stage with little resistance.

In some situations, when the law fails to discipline the general public, it can be effective to deal with a specific individual as a means of sending a warning. This serves to encourage compliance and obedience from others.

This story also connects to the saying, "Knock the tiger, and the alert will be awesome." This phrase metaphorically illustrates asserting dominance and instilling fear in others. By knocking on the beam, one demonstrates their power and intimidating attitude towards the tiger. It serves as a display of strength, unpredictability, and the potential consequences for defiance. The message conveyed is that if one does not comply or submit honestly, they may face severe consequences, even being killed and eaten.

In the military context, this tactic refers to the stratagem of commanding and establishing authority through various means of warning, inducement, and suggestion. Its purpose is to unify the will and actions of subordinates, prevent disobedience, and control weak enemies without direct military confrontation. By covertly using warnings, accusations, and firm attitudes, relevant individuals are compelled and influenced. This method enables the transmission of information, the establishment of authority, and the control of people.

The metaphorical meaning of this stratagem can be understood from two perspectives. Firstly, in military actions, it involves using political and diplomatic strategies to apply pressure, cooperate, and employ warning and inducement. This approach can lead to victory without engaging in direct combat against a weaker opponent, or using implied attacks against a stronger opponent.

Secondly, it entails the tactic of using the punishment of one individual to scare others and enforce obedience. It involves dealing with smaller matters to warn and deter those with greater influence. In certain situations where it is difficult to enforce punishment universally, dealing with a single person can serve as a warning to the broader public, setting an example for others. This indirect method of warning and subduing is employed when it is impractical or inconvenient to directly "scold" the intended target. It allows for the expression of blame or dissatisfaction in a circuitous but impactful manner.

In the military realm, this tactic is observed when commanding numerous subordinates, ensuring cohesion within the organization, and preventing orders or prohibitions from being disregarded. It is also utilized when dealing with weaker enemies to subdue them without engaging in direct military confrontation, preventing them from seizing opportune moments to resist. Through covert means, such as excuses, warnings, or employing appropriate tough stances, this stratagem facilitates effective communication, the establishment of authority, and control over the population.

In business warfare, this stratagem can be applied to market competition. It involves praising certain products to attract consumers while simultaneously criticizing competing products in a covert manner, aiming to sway consumers to one's own side.

27.Feigning madness without becoming insane

Hide behind the mask of a fool, a drunk, or a madman to create confusion about your intentions and motivations. Lure your opponent into underestimating your ability until, overconfident, he drops his guard. Then you may attack.

Sometimes, when faced with a strong opponent or a dangerous situation, people adopt a stratagem of pretending to be foolish or ignorant for a period of time. This stratagem is often referred to as "pretending to be dumb and selling stupidity." It involves deliberately acting clueless or displaying unconventional behaviors to create the impression that one is unaware or incapable. However, beneath this facade, the person is actually very aware and clever.

This stratagem can be observed in various scenarios. For example, when a hunter wants to catch a tiger but cannot overpower it directly, they may dress up as a pig and imitate pig sounds to lure the tiger out. When the tiger approaches, the hunter unexpectedly attacks and captures it. By pretending to be a harmless pig, the hunter tricks the tiger into believing it has an easy meal, causing it to lower its guard and fall into the hunter's trap.

In historical accounts, Ji Kang, a notable writer and musician during the Southern Dynasties in China, used a similar stratagem to protect himself. Due to his political views and remarks, he was imprisoned. However, during his time in jail, Ji Kang pretended to be crazy and acted foolishly. His odd behaviors and remarks convinced others that he had lost his sanity. By playing the fool, Ji Kang avoided direct confrontation with the ruling authorities, thus safeguarding his life.

This stratagem of pretending ignorance or incompetence in order to deceive and wait for the right moment is not limited to military contexts. It can also be used in everyday life to navigate challenging situations or deal with powerful opponents. By temporarily concealing one's abilities or strengths, individuals can protect themselves and bide their time until they have a strategic advantage or opportunity to overcome their adversaries.

The key idea behind pretending not to know or act is that, despite outward appearances, the person is well aware of the situation and their own capabilities. They choose to temporarily hide their true abilities, often due to unfavorable circumstances or the need for patience. It is a tactic used to deceive opponents, paralyze them with false impression, and wait for the right moment to take action.

28.Pull down the ladder after ascent

With baits and deceptions, lure your enemy into treacherous terrain. Then cut off his lines of communication and avenue of escape. To save himself, he must fight both your own forces and the elements of nature.

The stratagem of "Pull down the ladder after ascent" is about luring the enemy into a trap and then cutting off their escape route. This technique can be used in military or strategic situations to force the enemy into submission or to gain an advantage over them.

The original intention of going to the house to take the ladder is to tempt people to climb the tall building, and then remove the ladder, so that they have no choice but to give in easily. Militarily, it refers to luring the enemy to take profits, luring the other side into deep trouble with interests, and then completely destroying it, leaving no way back. A trick to force him into submission. It means the same thing as crossing the bridge to dismantle the board and crossing the river to dismantle the bridge.

The stratagem of "Pull down the ladder after ascent"   is beneficial to lure the enemy into a trap. However, the enemy will not fall into the trap if he is only lured and made to give him some convenience. Therefore, you should first put a "ladder" for him, that is, deliberately give him convenience, and wait for the enemy to "go upstairs", that is, to enter the already laid "pocket" before removing the "ladder" and panic in the enemy.

In order to lure the enemy into the trap, we should try to lure him. Seduce, that is, throw bait; To cast bait accurately and effectively, we must know the enemy's nature and know the enemy's situation. Some people cast bait, which is the same as fishing. Fishing, you should know what fish love what food; Before you get off the hook, you often have to consider deciding what fish to catch and what bait to throw. Grass carp loves grass and baits grass; Black herring loves snails and feeds on snails; Carassius auratus loves earthworms, and baits them ... To lure the enemy, we should know what the enemy loves and consider what bait to lure. Enemies who are greedy by nature use wealth as bait; A dissolute and lewd enemy takes beauty as bait; The enemy who is eager for success takes my weakness as bait; Enemies who are greedy for fame take power as bait ... In short, they can only be lured to the bait if they are interested.

Use various methods to introduce the enemy and people into the encirclement we set in advance, and then quickly cut off the enemy's route completely, making it impossible to escape and never come back. The main purpose of cutting off the enemy's retreat is to make it "inseparable". Only by "inseparable" can it be completely wiped out, or by taking advantage of the "inseparable" situation, it will cause great psychological pressure on the enemy and force him to submit.

Break its aid. It is to cut off the enemy's front response and backup. This stratagem is also called encircling the enemy to help. The "aid" of attacking and aiding the enemy can also be understood as "logistics supply". After pushing the enemy to the location set by the enemy, cutting off the logistics supply of him and his friends is equivalent to "pulling off" the "ladder" that protects him and holds the fighting capacity, which puts them in a dilemma.

Going to the house to take the ladder can be used by the enemy to break the enemy's rear road, and it can also be used by me to let myself go forward without leaving a retreat.

When Xiang Yu, the general of Chu Kingdom., was fighting against Qin Kingdom's army , the morale of the Chu's army was low in the face of Qin Kingdom's strong defense, and some people suggested retreating. In order to encourage the soldiers to fight to the end, Xiang Yu ordered the pots and kettles on board to be smashed. After crossing the river, After crossing the river, they sank their warships did not leave a way out for themselves. When the soldiers saw that they did not advance, they would be killed by the enemy, so they had to fight bravely and finally won. The commander-in-chief entrusts the troops with tasks, like pulling off the ladder after climbing a mountain, so that they can only move forward and not backward; To lead the army into the vassal state, we should push them forward like pulling an arrow crossbow to shoot an arrow. In this way, the use of specific environment and specific conditions on people's specific impact will suddenly stimulate or tap people's potential, which is the purpose of this stratagem.

When we find that the enemy is expanding its power and planning to crush or annex us, we can use the stratagem of going to the house to take the ladder to save ourselves, and we can also use it to crush or annex the enemy's power.

Create some kind of illusion, make the enemy feel that it is a good time, and start to act. Cover up the trap in the illusion. If the enemy really takes action, it will definitely fall into the trap and go to failure.

Take the ladder on the house, and it can also be used with other schemes, such as closing the door to catch thieves after taking the ladder. The beauty of the scheme lies in its flexible use.

29.Deck the tree with bogus blossom

Tying silk blossoms on a dead tree gives the illusion that the tree is healthy. Through the use of artifice and disguise, make something of no value appear valuable; of no threat appear dangerous; of no use appear useful.

Can you believe that a tree that cannot naturally blossom can actually bloom? This tree, originally unable to bloom, can be artificially made to do so. By cutting colorful silk into flower shapes and attaching them to the tree, it becomes difficult for people who don't look closely to distinguish between the fake flowers and the real tree. The beautiful fake flowers and the real tree complement each other, creating a completely novel, ingenious, and lifelike illusion.

In an ancient fable, a fox stumbled upon a tiger's skin and decided to put it on, pretending to be a real tiger. When other animals saw the fox, they mistook it for a genuine tiger and ran away in fear. In its newfound disguise, the fox began to bully other animals. However, its deception was eventually exposed by a wise old cat. The fox's stratagem was to use the disguise to instill fear in the other animals, portraying itself as a powerful predator. This fable illustrates the essence of the stratagem at hand.

In life, when one finds oneself at a disadvantage, it is wise to learn from the fox and conceal one's true capabilities. It is about pretending to possess great strength and prowess, even in the face of clear weakness. This confuses the enemy and can lead to a surprising victory. In military terms, it refers to leveraging the momentum of others to bolster one's own power and subdue the enemy.

In situations where the enemy is stronger and we are weaker, and when under attack, our forces should utilize various methods and create illusions to enhance our momentum. This can confuse, divert, repel, or even annihilate the enemy.

Not only can we make trees that traditionally do not bloom appear to blossom, but we can also borrow other people's trees to achieve the same effect. This means utilizing other favorable conditions to make trees bloom and bear fruit on behalf of weaker ones.

The reason for borrowing trees to bloom is mainly because our own trees are too weak to blossom. This stratagem is commonly employed in military tactics. By leveraging the existing situation and utilizing other resources, we can create advantageous positions, increase potential, and expand influence. This approach is particularly useful when our own capabilities are insufficient to form a viable force alone.

To illustrate further, if one desires to have eggs, they must first raise chickens. But what if there are no chickens available? Borrowing other people's chickens to lay eggs becomes a valid stratagem. By leveraging existing resources, we can achieve what was previously unattainable without increasing our own investment.

30.turning from the guest into the host or Host and guest reversed
Usurp leadership in a situation where you are normally subordinate. Infiltrate your target. Initially, pretend to be a guest to be accepted, but develop from inside and become the owner later.

A dove bird occupied a magpie's nest and deceived other birds into thinking that the nest was their own. It is often used to describe someone occupying someone else's position, rights or resources, but also deceiving others.

The wife lives with another man in her husband's room, and the husband is kicked out of the house. Who is the owner of this house? Who is the foreigner?

In the waning days of the Sui Dynasty, Li Yuan sought to conquer the realm. Prior to firmly establishing his footing, he adopted a humble posture and sought refuge under the formidable Li Mi. However, Li Mi's complacency towards Li Yuan allowed him to gradually grow stronger, ultimately resulting in Li Mi being ousted from power instead.

Literally speaking, the terms "host" and "guest" represent a host-guest relationship. The host refers to someone who owns a place or entertains others, while the guest is someone who is invited or visits. In this relationship, the host usually provides hospitality, care, and attention, while the guest enjoys the treatment offered by the host and expresses respect and gratitude. This dynamic is commonly observed in various scenarios such as family, social gatherings, and business activities. The interaction and communication between hosts and guests often reflect politeness, respect, and a friendly relationship between them. However, what happens when the host seems more like a visiting guest in their own home? How should one handle a situation where the guest exercises the rights of the host?

By extension, the master is the sovereign, ruler, dominator, initiative, advanced and attacker, and is in a dominant position;

Guests are dependent, ruled, dominated, controlled, passive, followed by defenders, in a dominant position.

What should I do if the identity and status of the host and guest are reversed?

Anti-customer-oriented, it is the practice that the customer who is in the dominant position seizes the dominant position, replaces the original owner, and puts the original owner in the position of the customer and fiddles with it at will. Therefore, it is a transposition method, or a position-taking method.

In real life, horse riding or beard-gliding is quite popular. Of course, flattery is to get on the horse. If you get on the boss, you can easily manipulate your boss and make profits. This is a modern anti-customer-oriented technique. I wonder if those officials who are fond of flatterers have thought of this layer.

Anti-customer-oriented, used in the military, refers to the stratagem of changing passivity into initiative in war and struggle, and striving to master the initiative in war and struggle. To implement this stratagem, we should try our best to exploit loopholes, pin in, control its heads, organs or key parts, seize the favorable opportunity, and merge or control others.

31.The beauty trap; Use seductive women to corrupt the enemy
To use a beautiful woman to deceive the enemy, enticing them to indulge in pleasure and lose their will to fight.

After King GouJian of the Yue Kingdom was captured, he behaved submissively and flattered King FuChai of Wu in every possible way, gaining his trust and eventually being released back to the Yue Kingdom. To demonstrate his loyalty, GouJian selected two exceptionally beautiful women and presented them to FuChai. He also offered rare and valuable jewels to the King of Wu every year. FuChai believed that GouJian had fully submitted, and thus had no suspicions whatsoever. FuChai spent his days drinking and reveling with the beauties, completely ignoring the advice of his ministers. Later, FuChai became increasingly infatuated with the women, neglecting his duties and affairs of state. GouJian saw this and rejoiced in his heart. Eventually, the Yue Kingdom took advantage of the situation and successfully annihilated the State of Wu, forcing FuChai to commit suicide.

When the King of the Jin's Kingdom was preparing to conquer other countries, he first sent people to offer well-crafted knives and beautiful jade to the rulers of those countries. He also sent young and attractive singers and dancers to captivate the will of the enemy kings, causing them to neglect the governance of their kingdoms and relax their guard against the Jin's Kingdom. As a result, the Jin's Kingdom ultimately destroyed those states.

The so-called "beauty trap" is a stratagem that involves using beautiful women to deal with enemies. The desire for beauty is inherent in human nature, and some people become infatuated with it. Some are willing to sacrifice wealth, status, and even morals, laws, and principles in order to obtain beauty. The use of beautiful women in military stratagem has long been utilized as an important tactic for defeating enemies.

The purpose of the "beauty trap" is to demoralize the enemy and sap their determination. However, the "beautiful women" used in this stratagem are just auxiliary means to achieve military objectives. When facing obstacles or difficulties, it is necessary to eliminate those who pose a hindrance, win over and corrupt the enemy, and turn them to one's advantage. It is not effective for everyone and only works on the weak-willed. The success of the tactic depends on its acceptance by the target. The "beautiful women" are merely external factors; their effectiveness relies on internal factors.

Send your enemy beautiful women to cause discord within his camp. This stratagem can work on three levels.

First, the ruler becomes so enamoured with the beauty that he neglects his duties and allows his vigilance to wane.

Second, other males at court will begin to display aggressive behaviour that inflames minor differences hindering co-operation and destroying morale.

Third, other females at court, motivated by jealousy and envy, begin to plot intrigues further exacerbating the situation.

For enemies whom it is difficult to conquer through military operations, one should use "sugar-coated bullets" to first defeat the enemy commanders mentally and destroy their fighting spirit, and then proceed with the attack. For powerful enemies, it is necessary to subdue their commanders; for cunning commanders, efforts should be made to corrode their loyalty by launching emotional attacks and softening their stance.

People often say, "Heroes cannot resist the allure of a beautiful woman." They also say, "Since ancient times, heroes have been fond of beauty; without this fondness, one cannot be a hero." Even heroes can be conquered and captivated by a beautiful woman, which demonstrates the immense power and appeal of beauty.

Thus, the use of beauty to deal with others, pursue interests, or achieve desires has continuously been employed, giving rise to various lively and vivid strategies known as "beauty traps". Beauty possesses more power than any weaponry. The use of force generates hatred and resistance, while beauty can erode the willpower of enemies, sap their physical strength, and provoke internal contradictions. With a flicker of seductive eyes, a graceful twist of the waist, or a gentle display of affection, even the strongest enemy is bound to crumble.

In diplomacy, beauty also holds significant leverage, surpassing armed confrontation and political threats.

In domestic governance, the beauty trap is also highly effective. Emperors often use it to strengthen their rule. Emperor's daughters never have trouble finding marriage partners, but in reality, there are specific criteria for their marriage: attracting talented individuals is a form of marriage that continuously buys hearts and recruits talents, while marrying the descendants of influential ministers is another form of marriage that consolidates the unity of the ruling group. If the emperor's biological daughters are all married off, there are always adoptive daughters available.

The subjects also understand the importance of beauty. Thus, they offer their daughters to emperors and even high-ranking officials and nobles, sometimes even offering their wives. If their wives and daughters are not attractive, they can be replaced with beautiful ones. Consequently, they win the favor of the emperor, who rewards the officials' titles, land, or allows them to assert power over the country. This situation is commonly referred to as "connections through women's relationships."

This stratagem should not be limited to understanding beauty as a mere medium for deception. Means, items, and interests that can mislead others, trapping them in indulgence and abandoning principles can also be considered alternative forms of the beauty trap.

32.presenting a bold front to conceal unpreparedness or Empty city ploy

When the enemy is superior in numbers and your situation is such that you expect to be overrun at any moment, then drop all pretense of military preparedness, act calmly and taunt the enemy, so that the enemy will think you have a huge ambush hidden for them.

It works best by acting calm and at ease when your enemy expects you to be tense.

This is a psychological warfare tactic. When our forces are unable to confront the enemy and are trapped inside the city, intentionally opening the city gates can induce doubts in the enemy's mind, making them fear that there might be an ambush inside the city. This feigned confusion disturbs the enemy's judgment, leading them to voluntarily retreat and resolve the crisis. However, this method is a last resort, as if the enemy sees through the ruse, it could result in the complete annihilation of our entire army.

The "Empty City stratagem" is a particularly remarkable tactic that has been widely discussed and admired, especially in the novel "Romance of the Three Kingdoms."

The story of Zhuge Liang using the Empty City stratagem to scare away the massive army led by Sima Yi is the most typical example. Zhuge Liang stationed his troops in YangPing Pass and sent the majority of his forces to attack the enemy, leaving only a small number of weak and elderly soldiers behind in the city. Suddenly, news arrived that Sima Yi, the commander of the Wei army, was leading 150,000 troops to attack the city. Despite the danger, Zhuge Liang remained unfazed. He ordered the city gates to be wide open and sent people to sweep and sprinkle water at the city entrance. Zhuge Liang himself climbed up the city tower, calmly sat down, played the zither, and maintained a composed attitude.

Zhuge Liang had no prominent generals by his side, only a group of civilian officials. Half of the 5,000 troops under his command were away transporting supplies, leaving only around 2,000 soldiers in the city. When the news of Sima Yi's arrival reached everyone, they were all shocked and fearful. Zhuge Liang, standing on the city tower, commanded them: "Hide all the flags, and do not move from your positions. Anyone who goes out without permission or causes a disturbance will be beheaded. Open all four city gates, with twenty soldiers at each gate disguised as ordinary people, sweeping the streets and sprinkling water. When the Wei army arrives, no one should act on their own. I have a stratagem." Zhuge Liang himself wore a crane robe, a tall official hat, took two young boys with him, and brought a zither to the city wall. He sat down, burning incense, and slowly began to play the zither.

When Sima Yi's vanguard troops arrived at the city, they saw this formidable show and did not dare to enter the city easily. They quickly returned to report to Sima Yi. After hearing the report, Sima Yi smiled and said, "How could this be possible?" He then ordered the entire army to halt and personally rode forward to take a look. Not far from the city, he indeed saw Zhuge Liang sitting on the city tower, with a smile on his face, playing the zither. There was a young boy holding a sword on his left side, and another young boy holding a dust brush on his right side. Inside and outside the city gates, there were more than twenty people disguised as commoners, diligently sweeping the streets with their heads down, as if no one else was around.

After seeing this, Sima Yi became suspicious and had doubts, fearing that there might be an ambush inside the city. Therefore, he did not dare to rashly enter the city and ordered his troops to retreat. His son asked, "Could it be that Zhuge Liang really has no soldiers in the city, so he purposely created this scene? Father, why are we retreating?" Sima Yi replied, "Zhuge Liang is always cautious and never takes risks. Now that the city gates are wide open, there must be an ambush inside. If our army enters, we will fall into their trap. Let's quickly retreat!" As a result, all the troops withdrew.

The key to using this tactic is to have a clear understanding of the psychological state and characteristics of the enemy's generals. Zhuge Liang used the Empty City stratagem to resolve the crisis because he had a thorough understanding of Sima Yi's cautious and suspicious nature, allowing him to take such a risky stratagem.

By intentionally revealing our weak military strength and displaying this vulnerability to the enemy, creating uncertainty and doubts about our actual capabilities. In a situation where the balance of power is greatly tilted in favor of the enemy, using "deception in emptiness" as a psychological tactic allows us to halt or thwart the enemy's offensive, gaining time to search for opportunities.

The "empty city stratagem" is not specifically designed to make opponents unaware of their own strength. Rather, it is a tactic used to deceive and confuse the enemy by creating an appearance of vulnerability. It does not aim to cover up the defender's true capabilities but rather to manipulate the enemy's perception and decision-making process.

During the Gulf War, which began on January 17th, 1991, the multinational forces led by the United States conducted air strikes against Iraq for 38 days. The Iraqi government organized extensive civil defense mobilization with the aim of protecting their war potential. Throughout the war, the Iraqi army and civilians employed various measures such as deception and the creation of obstacles to confuse the enemy and achieve comprehensive protection.

In preparation for the war, Iraq managed to obtain satellite images of important domestic targets taken by France through purchase. Based on this information, they carried out targeted camouflage and terrain modifications for vital locations like Baghdad. Additionally, Iraq procured plastic weapon models from different countries. During the conflict, the Iraqi army utilized these models, along with a large number of fake planes, missiles, and tanks made of wood and plastic, to create false targets. The intention was to mislead and confuse the multinational forces.

Furthermore, the Iraqi army employed tactics like burning waste rubber tires around airports and other strategic sites, blowing sand, and spraying water to obscure the targets and disrupt the detection and guidance systems of air raid weapons used by the multinational forces. These measures played a role in safeguarding the safety of real targets.

Overall, these tactics employed by Iraqi forces during the Gulf War were aimed at deceiving and confusing the enemy rather than covering up their true strength.

33.Sow discord among the enemy; Use double agent

Undermine your enemy's ability to fight by secretly causing discord between him and his friends, allies, advisors, family, commanders, soldiers, and population.

While he is preoccupied settling internal disputes, his ability to attack or defend is compromised.

An ignorant child is innocent and naive. As long as you play along with their characteristics and entertain them, you can easily manipulate them and get them to obey you. If someone is harmed, it is usually due to some external force they are unable to resist. By exploiting this common knowledge, one can harm themselves, but if they can make it seem real and convince their enemies, they can execute a divide and conquer stratagem. This is similar to deceiving a child, deceiving the enemy to manipulate them to our advantage.

The use of spies to spread false intelligence for the purpose of sowing division is a stratagem commonly employed. Spies are individuals who create suspicion and mistrust among the enemy forces, while counterintelligence involves using enemy spies to sow dissension among their own ranks.

In the stratagem of "planting doubts within their suspicions," false intelligence is spread using enemy spies embedded within our own ranks. By doing so, we undermine the enemy's confidence and gain support from within their own forces. This approach avoids direct confrontation and minimizes the risk of failure, as it leverages the enemy's own trust in their spies.

Counterintelligence involves turning enemy spies to our advantage. This can be achieved by utilizing the information obtained from infiltrating enemy spies or through bribery. We can either use them directly for our benefit or intentionally leak false information for them to carry back to confuse the enemy's perception and disrupt their understanding of our true situation.

However, it is important to note that bribing enemy spies may not always be a foolproof stratagem. If we can buy them with a large sum of money, chances are they can also be bought by others at an even higher price, making us susceptible to deception and manipulation.

To manipulate enemy spies for our own advantage is a stratagem known as "using the enemy's own tactics against them."

Enemy spies are sent to gather intelligence and set traps for us. In response, we use the traps set by the enemy to further confuse them. This tactic involves using the enemy's own agents to deceive themselves, using their own resources against them. Many spies are motivated by financial gain, and they will serve whoever pays them the most. If we can offer a more enticing offer than the enemy, the spy may choose to work for us instead. Therefore, the primary method of manipulating enemy spies is through generous bribes. We can also pretend to be unaware and intentionally leak false information to them, turning the enemy's spies to our advantage. Another approach is to sow discord and create conflicts among enemy ranks, creating divisions and destroying their unity, turning them against each other. If the enemy remains united, they become a formidable force that is difficult to defeat. Therefore, the goal of division and manipulation is to fundamentally separate the enemy at a psychological level.

By turning the traps set by the enemy against them, we are employing the stratagem of "using the enemy's own tactics against them." Simply put, it means using the enemy's own agents to confuse themselves, causing self-inflicted harm. It is akin to using the enemy's own hand to smack themselves in the face, inflicting damage onto themselves.

34.Deceiving the enemy by torturing one's own man

Pretending to be injured has two possible applications. In the first, the enemy is lulled into relaxing his guard since he no longer considers you to be an immediate threat.

The second is a way of ingratiating yourself to your enemy by pretending the injury was caused by a mutual enemy.

Translate to English: The "Deceiving the enemy by torturing one's own man" stratagem refers to a remarkable incident during the Three

Kingdoms period in ancient China. Huang Gai, a renowned general from the Kingdom of Wu, volunteered to participate in a staged act with Zhou Yu. In this act, Zhou Yu pretended to beat Huang Gai severely, and afterwards, Huang Gai used this as an excuse to express his willingness to surrender to Cao Cao, the enemy commander. Meanwhile, Cao Cao's undercover agent within the ranks of the Kingdom of Wu reported the incident of Huang Gai being beaten. Despite Cao Cao's shrewdness, he did not anticipate that Huang Gai's injuries were genuine while his surrender was a ruse. As a result, Cao Cao easily believed Huang Gai.

Consequently, during the Battle of Red Cliffs, when Cao Cao saw Huang Gai leading a fleet of about ten small boats towards him, he did not suspect a thing. He assumed it was part of Huang Gai's plan of infiltrating from within as mentioned in his surrender letter. However, to his surprise, as soon as they met, Huang Gai commanded his soldiers to ignite the small boats filled with straw, oil, and grease, taking advantage of the wind to set Cao Cao's fleet on fire. Countless casualties were inflicted upon the Wei forces, and Cao Cao suffered a major defeat, escaping with great embarrassment back to the north.

This stratagem became famous not only for its tactical execution but also because the experienced general Huang Gai was willing to sacrifice his personal interests in order to gain Cao Cao's trust by enduring humiliation and beatings. This ultimately turned the tide of the battle, saving the nation and its people from imminent danger. Huang Gai's courage is admirable, and his selflessness in sacrificing personal gains for the greater good is commendable. Thus, the "Ku Rou Ji" stratagem not only brought fame to Zhuge Liang and Zhou Yu for their strategic prowess but also elevated Huang Gai's life to a higher level of moral integrity, where he was willing to sacrifice personal interests for the greater cause.

In order to assassinate the enemy leader, the assassin reluctantly killed his wife and children to express his loyalty to the enemy leader. After the successful assassination, he refused the reward and asked to be buried in the same place as his wife and children after committing suicide.

The bitter stratagem is to first torture oneself, using blood and tears to get close to the enemy, while secretly carrying out subversive activities. The purpose of taking risks is to gain the enemy's trust through deception. This stratagem is actually a deviation from a special practice.

In order to bring real drug dealers to justice, the police do not hesitate to go undercover, deep into the middle of drug dealers, pretending to be drug dealers, and experiencing drug trafficking and drug testing in order to gain their trust.

Risks are not only used in wars but are also widely seen in all fields of social life. Be careful when using this method because the implementation of risks involves self-harm, which can be very painful. Even if it succeeds, the fruit of victory also contains blood and tears. A bitter pill is not only "bitter" but also "risky." If the enemy is hard-hearted or resourceful, it is not easy to take the bait. Once this stratagem is discovered, not only will the pain of self-harm be endured in vain, but even life will be lost. Therefore, whenever possible, try not to use this method.

35.coordinating one stratagem with another or Interlocking stratagems

In important matters, one should use several Stratagems applied simultaneously after another as in a chain of Stratagems. Keep different plans operating in an overall scheme; however, in this manner if any one stratagem fails, then the chain breaks and the whole scheme fails.

Near Dr. Swift's house lived a wealthy old woman who often sent her servant to deliver gifts to him. Dr. Swift accepted the gifts but never gave any reward to the servant. One day, while Dr. Swift was busy writing, the servant rushed into his room and threw a package on the desk, saying, "My master sent you two rabbits." Annoyed, Dr. Swift turned around and said, "Child, that's not how you present a package. Now, sit in my seat and see how I do it, and remember this lesson."

The obedient servant sat in the chair as instructed while Dr. Swift left the room. He then knocked on the door and waited for the servant's response. Hearing the servant say, "Come in," he quietly entered the room and approached the table, saying, "Sir, my mistress sends her warm regards and hopes that you accept these two rabbits." The servant smiled and replied, "Thank you, and please convey my gratitude to your mistress for her kindness. Also, these two shillings are a reward for you personally."

Dr. Swift was taken aback and realized that he had never given any tip to this hardworking servant. Apologetically, he smiled and nodded. From then on, he never forgot to give a tip to the servant.

In Western culture, tipping is a way to express gratitude and encouragement for someone's assistance. Dr. Swift had overlooked this detail due to his preoccupation with his studies, which made the servant unhappy. However, if the servant had demanded a tip directly, it would have put him in an awkward position and could have affected his image in Dr. Swift's eyes. Therefore, the clever servant employed a "chain of events" .He first provoked Dr. Swift's displeasure with his rude behavior, prompting Dr. Swift to offer a demonstration of proper etiquette. Then, by "cooperating" with Dr. Swift's performance, he brought the issue of tipping to the forefront, reminding Dr. Swift of his obligation. This stratagem effectively protected Dr. Swift's reputation while achieving the servant's goal.

During the Song Dynasty, a general once used a series of tactics to defeat The army of the Jin dynasty. He analyzed that the Jin dynasty soldiers were formidable, especially their cavalry, which was exceptionally brave. Directly engaging them in battle would cause significant casualties to his soldiers. Therefore, he advocated for capturing the enemy's major weaknesses, finding ways to restrain them, and seeking good opportunities for battle.

Once, his troops encountered the Jin's army again, and he immediately ordered his troops not to engage in direct combat with the enemy but to adopt guerrilla tactics. Whenever the enemy advanced, he ordered his troops to retreat. As soon as the enemy settled down, he ordered an attack. When the Jin's army counterattacked with full force, he led his troops to disappear without a trace. In this way, retreating and advancing, attacking and stopping, he exhausted the Jin's army. They wanted to fight but couldn't find a way to do so.

At night, the Jin's soldiers were exhausted and ready to return to their camp for rest. At this point, he secretly sprinkled black beans cooked with spices on the ground and used this to launch a surprise attack on the Jin's army. The Jin's army had no choice but to fight back with all their might. Once again, his troops encountered the Jin's army and deliberately pretended to retreat. The Jin's army was furious and chased after them.

The Jin's army's horses ran around all day, hungry and thirsty. They smelled the food on the ground and knew that it was something that could fill their stomachs. They rushed to eat the black beans and refused to move forward even when beaten with whips by soldiers. The Jin's army couldn't control their horses, and in the dark, they became very chaotic. At this time, the Song general gathered all his troops and surrounded them from all sides, killing the Jin's soldiers and achieving a complete victory for the Song army.

A series of Stratagems is to confuse the enemy's judgment with one stratagem and then attack them with another stratagem, so as to create internal conflicts and achieve the goal of defeating the enemy. It can also be a combination of multiple interlocking meters. No matter how strong the enemy is, we can defeat them through this stratagem.

36.Run away to fight another day, Escape is the best policy.

If it becomes obvious that your current course of action will lead to defeat, then retreat and regroup. When your side is losing, there are only three choices remaining: surrender, compromise, or escape.

Surrender is complete defeat, compromise is half defeat, but escape is not defeat.

As long as you are not defeated, you still have a chance. This is the most famous of the Strategies, immortalized in the form of a Chinese idiomidiom Of " Thirty-Six Strategies, fleeing is best".

When facing a powerful enemy, what should you do? Keep fighting until you run out of ammunition and die in battle? Or should you retreat first and then think of a better way? The best policy is to escape. Don't meet the enemy head-on. If the enemy is strong and we are weak, it is like a head fighting against an egg. If we fight hard against it, our heads will be broken, but the enemy will not suffer too much.

Why should we lose and end up in failure?

In ancient China, the Song army fought against a strong enemy. The Song generals withdrew all of their troops in the evening, leaving only flags flying in front of the barracks. They hung them up in advance, put their front legs on the floor, and knocked them. The enemy soldiers didn't notice it, so they held each other for a whole day. When they found that the situation was abnormal, the Song army was already far away. This can be called a good example of retreat.

Retreating is not always the wisest stratagem, but when the situation is very dangerous, it is just right to go and make people feel smart. When your favorite person doesn't love you anymore, it is unwise to hold on to it. When you learn to give up, you will learn to be mature.

When doing scientific research, if the research direction is proved to be wrong, you cannot go all the way to the dark. Giving up properly is a kind of wisdom, a kind of stratagem, and an ability.

Militarily, when the enemy is strong and we are weak, we have several options: make peace, surrender, fight to the death, or retreat. Of these four choices, the first three are completely hopeless and a complete failure. Only the fourth option, retreat, can save strength and make a comeback. Therefore, "walking" is the best policy. In an unfavorable situation where there is a disparity between the enemy and ourselves, we should take the initiative to retreat in a planned way, avoid strong enemies, look for fighters, and make progress by retreating. This should also be the best policy in stratagem.

Leaders should be good at retreating from difficulties. If you already know that things can't be done, don't bite the bullet and do it. You should play it by ear and give up as soon as possible. Don't waste your time and energy. When our own strength is insufficient, we should avoid decisive battles with the enemy and first preserve our own strength. In the case of "avoiding everything", avoid it. "If you stay in the green hills, you will not worry about burning firewood." This is a stratagem to get out of danger.

The temporary concession made now is a means to strive for greater progress in the next step. In this case, "going" is not mainly because of the inability to do so but because of the need to seduce and mobilize the enemy. This is a circuitous tactic that takes detour as the straight line. By retreating in disguise, the enemy can be lured into depth, gathered, and annihilated.

We must seize the opportunity and rush back. When fighting the enemy, we should be good at observing the fighters so that we can advance and retreat without being blind or passive. Otherwise, we will only be ruined. Like Fan Li under the King of Yue, he would rather give up his splendor and live in the countryside. Why? Because there is no murder or hook. He is wise and a model who knows how to retreat quickly. However, it is easy to make a swift retreat, which requires us not only to be decisive but also to be brave and courageous. More importantly, we should be able to overcome our weaknesses, give up our vested interests, choose the right time, and hurry away so that the enemy cannot catch us.

BIBLIOGRAPHY

Stefan H. Verstappen. The Thirty-Six stratagems of Ancient China.First

Edition Published by China Books, SF 1999.ISBN 978-0-9869515-8-9
Luo Guanzhong. Romance of the Three Kingdoms .People's Literature
Publishing House,
China,2018.ISBN 978-7-0201255-5-5
Gao Mou, The Thirty-Six stratagems of shopping malls. Petroleum
Industry Press. China. In 1999 .ISBN 978-7-5021262-6-1

Thanks

Maxim Gorky once said that books are the stairway to human progress. In the vast sea of traditional Chinese cultural treasures, it has been quite a challenge for me to explain The Thirty-Six stratagems in a simple and understandable way. In order to spread human wisdom, and to allow friends from all over the world to read and appreciate this book, and understand the marvelous strategies within, I have spent a lot of time consulting with university professors and researchers in Chinese traditional culture. I sincerely thank them for their rigorous work style and enthusiastic guidance.

I would also like to express my gratitude to my wife. In order to ensure the smooth publication of this book, she has taken on the other responsibilities of our family, such as taking care of my daily meals and handling external affairs. Without the support and understanding of my family, this book would not have come into the world so quickly. It is because of my family's understanding that I am able to focus on accessing various information without any worries.

I would also like to thank my doctor. Writing requires long hours spent sitting at a desk, and on average, I spend 13 hours a day on writing. Apart from meals, my time is devoted solely to writing. This has resulted in back pain and blurred vision. Thanks to the care of my doctor friend, I have been able to complete this task with relative ease.

Lastly, I am grateful for the advancements in internet technology, which have made writing and accessing research materials much easier and more convenient.

About the author

KEN LEE is a writer, educator in China and a communicator of traditional culture in China. He used to be a high school teacher, educated and trained, and studied psychology. He is also a world traveler and has lived in Australia for many years. The blogger of the article has published many books about China's cultural customs.If you have any questions about reading, please send me an email, ateamystic@gmail.com.